T0320172

Work and Labor in American Popular Culture

Crisis and decline in the working class were frequent themes in American popular culture during the 1970s. In contrast, more positive narratives about America's managerial and professional class appeared during the 1980s. Focusing on these two key decades, this book explores how portrayals of social class and associated work and labor issues including gender and race appeared in specific films, television shows, and music. Comparing and contrasting how forms of popular media portrayed both unionized and non-unionized workers, the book discusses how workers' perceptions of themselves were in turn shaped by messages conveyed through media. The book opens with an introduction which outlines the historical context of the immediate post-war period and the heightened social, political, and economic tension of the Cold War era. Three substantial chapters then explore film, television, and music in turn, looking at key works including *Star Wars, Coming Home, 9 to 5, Good Times, The Mary Tyler Moore Show*, and the music of Bruce Springsteen and rap artists. Drawing on both primary and secondary sources, the book is principally situated within wider labor and working-class history research, and the relatively new history of capitalism historical sub-field. This book is vital reading for anyone interested in issues around labor and work in the media, labor history, and popular culture history during two key decades in modern American history.

Jason Russell, Ph.D., is a Professor of Labor Studies at SUNY Empire State University. He is the author of several books including *Canada, A Working History, Leading Progress: The Professional Institute of the Public Service of Canada, 1920–2020*, and *Management and Labor Conflict: An Introduction to the US and Canadian History.*

Global Perspectives on Work and Labor
Series editor: Jason Russell

Available Titles in this Series:

Work and Labor in American Popular Culture
Representation in Film, Music and Television in the 1970s and 1980s
Jason Russell

Work and Labor in American Popular Culture

Representation in Film, Music and Television in the 1970s and 1980s

Jason Russell

 Routledge
Taylor & Francis Group

NEW YORK AND LONDON

First published 2024
by Routledge
605 Third Avenue, New York, NY 10158

and by Routledge
4 Park Square, Milton Park, Abingdon, Oxon, OX14 4RN

Routledge is an imprint of the Taylor & Francis Group, an informa business

© 2024 Jason Russell

The right of Jason Russell to be identified as author of this work has been asserted in accordance with sections 77 and 78 of the Copyright, Designs and Patents Act 1988.

All rights reserved. No part of this book may be reprinted or reproduced or utilised in any form or by any electronic, mechanical, or other means, now known or hereafter invented, including photocopying and recording, or in any information storage or retrieval system, without permission in writing from the publishers.

Trademark notice: Product or corporate names may be trademarks or registered trademarks, and are used only for identification and explanation without intent to infringe.

ISBN: 978-1-032-47095-5 (hbk)
ISBN: 978-1-032-47101-3 (pbk)
ISBN: 978-1-003-38456-4 (ebk)

DOI: 10.4324/9781003384564

Typeset in Sabon
by MPS Limited, Dehradun

Contents

Acknowledgments

I want to thank everyone at Routledge for their assistance with this book, especially Brianna Ascher, Jessica Rech, and Andy Humphries. I grew up watching many of the films and television programs described in this analysis with my mother Trudy Warren, so this book is for her. I hope that the book encourages readers to listen to music and watch television shows and films from the 1970s to 1980s, and hopefully learn something about American working life during those years.

Introduction

Whether sitting in a movie theater, reclining in front of a television, or listening to music through any number of devices, work and labor is a key part of popular media in the United States. Work has been the subject of many films, television series, and works of music. People may not always hear the messages that media creators send about working life, but those messages are nonetheless present. This book is an introduction to how work and labor themes were incorporated into film, television, and music in the 1970s and 1980s. Those decades were periods of change as Americans tried to move beyond the tumultuous 1960s. The country experienced social, economic, and political change in the 1970s that culminated in the triumph of modern conservatism with the election of Ronald Reagan in 1980 and on to the end of the Cold War. Wages stopped rising to meet increases in the cost of living, stagflation took hold of the US economy following the 1973 embargo mounted by the Organization of the Petroleum Exporting Countries, the political right became ascendant politically, and American unions experienced a significant decline.[1]

This book is intended to be an introductory overview and it references key films, TV programs, and popular music where work and labor were integrated by the people who created them. It addresses three questions: how was work and labor depicted in film, TV, and music, who created the entertainment content, and what messages were conveyed in it? It is organized into this introduction, three chapters, and a conclusion. The chapters, respectively, examine film, television, and music. Every chapter is further sub-divided by genre or theme, such as country and rock and roll for music. The overall analysis incorporates both primary and secondary source content. The book should be of use to American readers who want an accessible overview of representations of work and labor in popular media from 1970 to 1989 and will hopefully be of particular use to readers in other countries who have had less extensive access to American popular media than people in the

DOI: 10.4324/9781003384564-1

United States. There are several existing monographs on work and labor in American film, television, and music including work by Nystrom, Marcink, Greene, Arnold, and Echols and this book will hopefully add to them.[2]

The first chapter examines key films that were made during the 1970s and 1980s, and those films illustrated that a film can be about work and labor without necessarily being about specific labor struggles waged by organized workers, or by workers engaged in paid work. The 1970s are a historically important period in American filmmaking with people like Michael Cimino, Martin Scorsese, and Francis Ford Coppola making landmark films that also included work and labor themes. Scorsese gave the world psychotic taxi driver Travis Bickle, Coppola based deranged Colonel Walter Kurtz on the work of author Joseph Conrad, and Cimino took a group of blue-collar steelworkers from outside of Pittsburgh to Vietnam and back. The working-class experience was evident in 1970s films beyond the work of Scorsese, Cimino, and Coppola and work and labor occasionally appeared in unexpected settings. George Lucas revolutionized science fiction in his 1977 film *Star Wars*.[3] Work and industrial environments were part of the Star Wars film franchise, which was another aspect of it that differentiated the films from previous science fiction works.[4]

The 1970s saw film makers express interest in nostalgia for the immediate post-World War II decades. Lucas made a major contribution to it with *American Graffiti*, and Paramount released a blue-collar 1950s musical film called *Grease* in 1978.[5] Interest in nostalgia was shaped by anxiety some Americans felt about the state of their country in the 1970s. Many blue-collar workers had generally earned wages and benefits that met or exceeded the cost of living in the 1950s and 1960s, and otherwise earned incomes that moved them into the middle class. The United States seemed to dominate the world economically and culturally, but that paradigm changed in the eyes of many people as the country withdrew from Vietnam after waging an inconclusive war. Americans dealt with rise of 1960s counterculture, the necessary changes brought by the civil rights movement, and an economy that seemed stalled compared with the 1950s and 1960s. The threat of global nuclear war, a conflict which could still easily happen in the twenty-first century, was always present in popular discourse. The idea that the country was in decline due to internal and external threats also shaped the narratives of police and vigilante films.

Women's labor, both paid and unpaid, appeared in 1970s films such as *Norma Rae* starring Sally Field.[6] Films that actually talked about unions were still an exception in the Hollywood production schedule in the 1970s. *F.I.S.T* starring Sylvester Stallone was a period film about union activity, but there was a lack of sympathetic characters and storylines that included organized labor.[7] This is a contradictory aspect of Hollywood overall as the film and television industries are heavily unionized and workers are represented by often militant unions such as the Screen Actors Guild-American Federation of Television and Radio Artists (SAG-AFTRA), the Writers Guild of America (WGA), and the Directors Guild of America (DGA). The most obvious answer to the question of Hollywood's aversion to making a lot of overtly labor-themed films is that the studios and production companies are owned and run by shareholders and corporate executives, and those are two groups who are ill-disposed toward workers' rights.

The 1980s witnessed a shift in representations of workers on movie theater screens, as blue-collar workers faded into the background and professional and managerial workers moved into the foreground. Films like *Wall Street*, directed by Vietnam War veteran Oliver Stone, slightly pulled back the curtain that shrouded the machinations of *Wall Street* and the belief systems of people who worked in finance.[8] The problem of globalization and industrial job loss was a theme in *Gung Ho!* and *Roger & Me*.[9]

Television in the 1970s depicted working people and their daily lives. In fact, if the 1970s was the director's decade on film, it was the producer's decade on television. Much of this aspect of American television was due to the production work of Norman Lear. Lear gave the world Archie Bunker and George Jefferson and showed Black American workers on the job. The miniseries adaption of Alex Hailey's book *Roots* brought the legacy of unpaid, bonded, racialized work right into American living rooms.[10] The nostalgia aspect of 1970s American culture manifested itself through *Happy Days* and its spinoff programs.[11] Working women were depicted in shows such as *The Mary Tyler Moore Show* and *Alice*.[12]

The shift away from featuring the working class in storylines in favor of the middle class was as pronounced on television as it was on film. Medical dramas are perpetually popular on television, and 1980s dramas strove to depict the reality of working as a physician or other medical professional. Police and private investigator dramas veered from realistic to entirely escapist in the 1980s. TV networks and producers correctly identified that American viewers wanted a break from memories of Vietnam and stagflation in the 1970s and gave viewers content that took them away from their everyday lives.

Film and television genres stayed constant during the 1970s and 1980s, but the music industry saw considerable change with some genres remaining constant and others coming and going relatively quickly. Music is an entertainment form that became much more portable in the 1970s and 1980s with the possibility to listen at home, in a car, on the job, or even while walking since the Sony Walkman was created in 1979. Punk and disco rose and fell in the 1970s, and hip-hop came as the decade ended and inexorably grew in popularity.

Michael Moore was associated with the working class and left politics because of *Roger & Me* and work and labor themes were present in films by directors like Scorsese. Norman Lear and other producers showed work and labor on television screens. Bruce Springsteen became a Rock and Roll Pete Seeger and Woody Guthrie all in one in the late 1970s, and especially in 1984 with his album *Born in the U.S.A.* There were other musicians across all popular genres who talked about working life in their work, but Springsteen rose above them all when it came to songs about work and labor. Record companies seem to have been less resistant to songs about working life than their counterparts in the film and television industries. Their response was not because they possessed a greater sense of social justice, but rather because an album like *Born in the U.S.A.* sold millions of copies and generated enormous profits. As subsequent analysis will show, a lot of fans loved Springsteen's songs but did not always recognize what they were hearing. *Born in the U.S.A.* was also the first album released as a compact disc for commercial sale.[13]

Some of the creative content that filled films, TV, and music would not be considered socially and culturally acceptable in the twenty-first century. The 1970s in particular was a period when overt racial and sexist epithets and representations appeared on movie and TV screens and on radio. For instance, a 1980s hit song by British band Dire Straits included a term that is now considered homophobic. Media content from the 1970s and 1980s represents attitudes, beliefs, and practices prevalent during those periods and should be viewed within this context when looked at from the perspective of the third decade of the twenty-first century.

The 1970s and 1980s were also years when the study of work and labor grew in academia. Labor history flourished during this period, and in the American context began with the work of historians like David Montgomery, Herbert Gutman, and Melvyn Dubofsky. Harry Braverman published an enduring book on work alienation and degradation, and Michael Burawoy described the process whereby workplaces condition workers to accept capitalism.[14] Work and labor were found in popular media and were subjects of serious intellectual inquiry on university and college campuses. Students who learned something about American labor history could see and hear aspects of it when they turned on a TV set, bought a movie cinema ticket, or turned on a radio.[15]

The 1970s and 1980s were also years of considerable change in American workplaces, as well as increased conflict between unions and employers and corporations sought to push back against organized labor's post-war gains. Corporate America was aided by the

Republican Party in this effort, especially by the election of Ronald Reagan as president in 1980. Reagan began his first administration with a collective bargaining dispute with the Professional Air Traffic Controllers' Association (PATCO), and the dispute ended with the Reagan administration firing all of the striking PATCO members. Employers took this move as a signal that they too could take a harsher line with unionized workers.[16]

The American economy changed in the 1970s and 1980s as the country began to feel the impact of globalization. American industry felt increased pressure from overseas competitors, wages stopped rising to meet increased living costs, and jobs began to be moved to countries where workers could be paid much less than in the United States. Entire communities declined as traditional industries like automotive and steel closed plants and laid-off workers. New industries also began to rise, especially in California's Silicon Valley.

Women worked full-time in greater numbers in the 1970s and that trend continued into the 1980s. They rightfully expected to have access to career mobility and to be paid the same salaries as men. The Equal Rights Amendment was passed in Congress in 1972, although it has not become part of the US Constitution as it has yet to be ratified by a sufficient number of states to make it an actual constitutional amendment. Workers of color made advancements in the 1960s due to the civil rights movement and legislative changes like the 1964 Civil Rights Act, and they expected to be treated equally on the job.

There was continuity and change in how work and labor appeared across film, television, and music in the 1970s and 1978. The problems that beset American workers, especially those in blue-collar jobs, were depicted in content found in all three entertainment mediums. Movies, TV shows, and songs reflected what was happening in society and sometimes the content found in them shaped popular discourse. Work and labor were always there in those two decades.

Notes

1 US union density declined from just under 30 percent of the non-agricultural workforce in 1970 to 16.4 percent in 1989. See Leo Panitch and Don Swartz, *From Consent to Coercion: The Assault on Trade Union Freedoms, third edition* (Aurora, ON: Garamond, 2003), 245.
2 See Derek Nystrom, *Hard Hats, Rednecks, and Macho Men: Class in 1970s American Cinema* (Oxford: Oxford University Press, 2009); Robert A. Marcink, *The Working Class in American Film* (Amherst, NY: Cambria Press, 2011); Doyle Greene, *The American Worker on Film: A Critical History, 1909–1999* (Jefferson, NC: McFarland and Company, 2010); Gordon Arnold, *The Afterlife of America's War in Vietnam* (Jefferson, NC: McFarland and Company, 2006); Alice Echols, *Hot Stuff: Disco and the Remaking of American Culture* (New York: W.W. Norton and Company, 2010).

3 *Star Wars*, directed by George Lucas (1977; Los Angeles, CA: Twentieth-Century Fox).

4 Patrick Goldstein, "That '70s era: a decade of excess and film success," 3 June 2003, *Los Angeles Times*, https://www.latimes.com/archives/la-xpm-2003-jun-03-et-gold3-story.html.

5 *American Graffiti*, directed by George Lucas (1973; San Rafael, CA: Lucasfilm and San Franciso, CA: The Coppola Company); *Grease*, directed by Randal Kleiser (1978; Los Angeles, CA: Allan Carr Enterprises, Stigwood Group).

6 *Norma Rae*, directed by Martin Ritt (1979; Los Angeles, CA: Twentieth-Century Fox).

7 *F.I.S.T.*, directed by Norman Jewison (1978; Los Angeles, CA: United Artists).

8 *Wall Street*, directed by Oliver Stone (1987; Los Angeles, CA: Twentieth-Century Studios).

9 *Gung Ho!*, directed by Ron Howard (1986; Los Angeles, CA: Paramount) and *Roger & Me*, directed by Michael Moore (1989; Los Angeles, CA: Warner Brothers).

10 Hailey, Alex, *Roots: The Saga of an American Family* (New York: Doubleday, 1976).

11 *Happy Days*, produced by Garry Marshall (1974–1984; Los Angeles, CA: ABC).

12 *Mary Tyler Moore Show*, produced by James L. Brooks and Allan Burns (1970–1977; Los Angeles, CA: MTM Enterprises) and *Alice*, produced by R. S. Allen, William P. D'Angelo, Harvey Bullock, Thomas Kuhn, and David Susskind (1976–1985; Los Angeles, CA: Warner Brother Television).

13 Bruce Springsteen, *Born in the U.S.A.*, Columbia 88875014281 1984, compact disc.

14 Harry Braverman, *Labor and Monopoly Capital: The Degradation of Work in the Twentieth Century* (New York: Monthly Review Press, 1974); Michael Burawoy, *Manufacturing Consent: Changes in the Labor Process Under Monopoly Capitalism* (Chicago: University of Chicago Press, 1979).

15 See David Montgomery, *The Fall of the House of Labor: The Workplace, the State, and American Labor Activism, 1865–1925* (Cambridge: Cambridge University Press, 1987); Herbert Gutman, *Work, Culture, and Society in Industrializing America: Essays in American Working-Class and Social History* (New York: Knopf, 1976); Melvyn Dubofsky, *We Shall Be All: A History of the Industrial Workers of the World* (New York: Quadrangle Books, 1969).

16 On the PATCO strike see Joseph McCartin, *Collision Course: Ronald Reagan, The Air Traffic Controllers, and the Strike That Changed America* (Oxford: Oxford University Press, 2011).

1 Film

Work and labor in their different forms were found in many important films in the 1970s and 1980s, and not always in ways that were entirely overt. The work performed by film characters was often central to a film's narrative, but few films focused directly on labor and workplace conflict. There are some key influences on how work and labor were portrayed during the 1970s and 1980s, including socio-economic change and the creative interests of the people making films. Movie studios were struggling to adapt to changes in audience tastes. Several expensive 1960s productions including *Cleopatra* lost money. The studios had been worried about losing viewers to television since that new medium went into widespread use in the 1950s, but a new generation of film directors and producers was beginning to make films that had greater market viability by the end of the 1960s.[1]

The 1970s became known for robust film making because of the impact of people like Francis Ford Coppola, Martin Scorsese, Terrence Malik, and Michael Cimino and it became known as a director's decade. Some genres waxed during that decade while others waned. Westerns, which were popular during the 1960s and preceding decades, fell out of favor with viewing audiences. Films focusing on grittier, often urban stories became more popular. America's Vietnam War experience influenced film making and was the topic of several films in the 1970s and 1980s. The reality of work and labor in 1970s and 1980s America was reflected in many key films, but depictions tended to focus on white male characters and much less on women and people of color. Working-class, middle-class, and professional workers appeared in films throughout both decades. Corporate leaders and managers also occasionally appeared as film characters.[2]

Films were principally made by well-established production companies in Hollywood such as Warner Brothers and Paramount, but executives at those firms produced some films with trepidation as they were different from movies that had come before them. Business leaders

DOI: 10.4324/9781003384564-2

are ever interested in stable profits, and while concerned about declining box office receipts, were loathe to deviate from what they regarded as proven movie formats. For example, war films were popular with studios as long as they were not expensive to produce and were made about wars that the United States won. Expensive films about the problematic consequences of war were less favored by the studios and by the viewing public.

This chapter will not focus on every film produced in the United States in the 1970s and 1980s that included work and labor themes and will instead focus on key productions that were made during those decades. It will describe films that depicted both contemporary and historical issues. Work and labor appeared in films that had lasting influence in popular culture, but not always in an overt manner. Film makers chose how work and labor would be depicted, with some experiences being more privileged than others.

The 1970s

Counterculture, Vietnam, and the Working Class

The United States experienced significant social change as the 1970s began. The counterculture movement that was prominently featured in late 1960s films like *Easy Rider* had never been as socially prominent as media representations of it may have suggested.[3] As Jefferson Cowie argued, there were still a lot of men with crew cuts and women with beehive hairdos in the 1970s who went to see Elvis Presley, which is a comment on nostalgia in post-war America.[4] There was interest in looking back before the 1960s to the 1950s. *Easy Rider* represented a major change in how the American working class was depicted, and a line can be readily drawn between it and John Ford's 1940 film adaption of John Steinbeck's book *The Grapes of Wrath*.[5] Ford's film depicted a repressed working class forming alliances and striving to overcome adversity, while *Easy Rider* shows a resentful and alienated working class.

Easy Rider depicted three characters played by Dennis Hopper, Jack Nicholson, and Peter Fonda as they rode their motorcycles across the United States before ultimately meeting their deaths at the hands of characters who could well have been the descendants of the Joad family from *The Grapes of Wrath*. Dennis Hopper directed *Easy Rider* and this film was in many ways the start of the director's decade, even though it came up one year before the 1970s started. It was an entirely fictional film, but the 1970s started with a film that was based on real events.

In the 1970 film *Joe,* Susan Sarandon, and Peter Boyle starred in a dark comedy that revolved around a murder, while also being written on class lines. Boyle's character, Joe Curran, is a factory worker who despises hippies and Sarandon's Melissa comes from a wealthy family.

Boyle is falsely convicted of murder and the scenario depicted in the film unexpectedly mirrored a mass murder that occurred in Detroit, Michigan weeks before the film premiered. *Joe* is not well-remembered in twenty-first-century America, outside of perhaps the community of film critics and afficionados, but subsequent films with similar themes would have a more lasting influence.[6]

Alienation fueled feelings of resentment and powerlessness, and the early 1970s provided tangible symbols for the working class to dislike and against which white blue-collar workers could feel themselves opposed. Vietnam, counterculture, and the Civil Rights Movement were often opposed by the white working class. For instance, the so-called Hard Hat riot of 1970 involved conservative unionized construction workers in New York City attacking antiwar protestors. Media portrayals of support or opposition to the war frequently focused on white Americans rather than Blacks or Latinos. The construction workers who participated in the New York City riot were white.[7]

The Vietnam War was fought on class lines. The United States introduced a military draft in 1940 with the passage of the Selective Training and Service Act of 1940. It would stay in effect until 1973 following the adoption of recommendations made by the President's Commission on an All-Volunteer Armed Force, which was otherwise known as the Gates Commission. The existence of the draft for 33 years from 1940 to 1973 brought profound social and cultural consequences to the United States, and it was reflected in film and other forms of popular media. There were instances when the draft helped raise interest in the media and accentuated patriotic feelings, such as when a celebrity like Elvis Presley answered a draft notice and showed up at an army depot to be inducted into military service. There were also instances when the draft drew negative attention to military service, such as when boxer Muhammad Ali refused to enlist after receiving a draft notice.[8]

Registering with the Selective Service system was a legal requirement, and still is in the third decade of the twenty-first century for American males aged 18–25. The draft is no longer a legal requirement, but the system underlying it remains in case the military feels it necessary to reintroduce one. Compulsory military service was introduced in the United States during World War I, and more importantly during the Civil War. Systems of compulsory service were rife with abuse and full of loopholes that could be readily exploited by people with the means and social status to do so. This was certainly the case during Vietnam, and resentment over who was made to serve and who was able to avoid combat service drove working-class animosity.

The American militaries that fought in both world wars, Korea, and Vietnam were working class, principally white, and overwhelmingly male. The key difference between Vietnam and the other conflicts was that the world wars and Korea were conflicts in which America prevailed. The United States suffered higher casualties in the world wars that it did in Vietnam— losses in Korea were actually lower than the 58,220 who died in Vietnam— but fighting in South-East Asia was entirely different than those earlier conflicts. The United States first entered the war by supporting France's efforts to maintain colonial control of Vietnam, it gradually escalated military aid to the South Vietnamese government, and President Lyndon Johnson formally deployed combat troops following the 1964 adoption of the Tonkin Gulf resolution by the US Congress. There was no formal declaration of war as there was with the world wars, no clearly defined front line, and an ill-defined war aim other than to keep South Vietnam from falling to Communism.[9]

Few films were made about the Vietnam War while the United States was actually engaged in it, although there were some notable exceptions. Robert Altman's 1970 film *M*A*S*H.* is perhaps the most notable example of a film about Vietnam, although it was set in the Korean War.[10] Based on a 1968 novel by Richard Hooker, it featured a large cast including Donald Sutherland, Eliot Gould, and Sally Kellerman who were cast as medical personnel in a mobile army surgical hospital.[11] The film was the inspiration for a television program that ran for long period in the 1970s and early 1980s, which was of course a much longer period than the United States was actually engaged in Korea.[12]

M*A*S*H. was a comedy—the television series even more so—but also dealt with matters of grief and loss, class, race, gender, and why the United States was fighting in Korea. The main characters worked as physicians and nurses, with combat troops coming through injured. Their lives were not at all romanticized. Only one character—Major Frank Burns played by Robert Duvall—espoused traditional views about America's role abroad and service in the military. In the film, Burns eventually suffers a breakdown. Getting such a film made that was actually set in Vietnam would have been difficult in 1970, and Americans knew the real meaning of what they were seeing in *M*A*S*H.* It was ultimately an antiwar film made at a time when the United States was engaged in a military quagmire that had little domestic support. *M*A*S*H.* was also an example of the new films that came out during the 1970s that reflected new trends in American film, with its combination of humor and cynicism about life in the United States and its policies abroad. There were still people in Hollywood who took a more established view of America's role abroad.

Hollywood had long supported official US government wartime policy through film production, but only one major production overtly supported American involvement in Vietnam. *The Green Berets* starred

John Wayne and came out in 1968, which was also the peak of US military involvement in the country. The film was shot in and around Fort Benning in Georgia, and Wayne co-directed it. The premise of the film revolved around a journalist played by David Janssen who was cynical about the war and who then travels to South Vietnam. The character, Beckworth, changes his opinion of America's presence after witnessing the conflict in person.[13]

The Green Berets did not depict the backstories of the characters, and instead entirely focused on their presence in South Vietnam. Wayne was known for roles in war films and westerns, and *The Green Berets* can be viewed as an effort to hold back the tide of critical films that would soon appear about the war. *The Green Berets* received negative reviews but did well at the box office. It was the kind of film that appealed to traditional white, working-class views of America's role in the world and not the type meant for anyone involved in counterculture.

The United States shifted from a direct combat role in Vietnam immediately after Richard Nixon became president in 1969, and completely withdrew combat troops in 1973. American efforts to support the South Vietnamese government and military failed. The South Vietnamese capital—Saigon—fell to the North Vietnamese in 1975. The American public was entirely ready to move on from the war, and few films were made about it in the early 1970s. Elia Kazan, who was notorious for naming eight suspected Communists during testimony before the House Committee on Un-American Activities (HUAC) in 1952, directed a violent 1972 film called *The Visitors*. That film focused on three Vietnam veterans who have returned to the United States. Kazan's film did not make a lasting impact on the Vietnam War film genre despite his notoriety as a director.[14]

The key wave of American films that focused on the war began in 1978 with *The Deer Hunter*, which referenced the white working-class experience in the war. They were also made by directors and actors who were much different than John Wayne. *The Deer Hunter* was one of a handful of films made during the 1970s and early 1980s that were long, often in excess of three hours, yet still drew large audiences into theaters. *The Deer Hunter* focused on the lives of three American steelworkers from Pennsylvania who volunteered for service overseas. It was directed by Michael Cimino.[15]

Cimino's decision to situate the main three characters—played by Christopher Walken, Robert De Niro, and John Savage—in a Pennsylvania steel industry community drew a link between the working class and the military. The characters are eager to get to Vietnam as quickly as possible, but De Niro is the only one who emerges comparatively unscathed by the experience. The film depicts the physical and psychological trauma of average working men who served in Vietnam and how they were viewed at home. *The Deer Hunter* is also unique in comparison to other Vietnam War films as it is set in both the United States and Vietnam. The other major Vietnam War film of 1978 was set entirely in the United States.

Coming Home revolves around characters played by Jane Fonda, Bruce Dern, and John Voight and was directed by Hal Ashby.[16] The political views of actors were not always well-known in the early 1970s unless they chose to publicly and vocally express them but Fonda was an exception as she opposed the Vietnam War and infamously visited Hanoi in 1972, where she actually posed with a North Vietnamese anti-aircraft gun.[17] She was subsequently derisively called Hanoi Jane in public and media discourse. She played the wife of a Marine Corps officer in *Coming Home*, and her character begins an extra-marital affair with a former high school love interest who also served in Vietnam and was paralyzed from the waist down. Dern played the husband while Voight was the partially paralyzed veteran.

The film principally drew attention because of the nudity and sexuality depicted in it, particularly one sexual act, but the overall theme of the film is of men returning home from the war irreparably damaged. Dern's character suffers emotional harm in Vietnam that is exacerbated by the realization that his wife has been unfaithful, while Voight's character has suffered permanent physical harm. *Coming Home* shared similarities with *The Deer Hunter*. There were female characters who did not know how to respond to the war experience of men who returned home, the problem of being back in the United States, and the lasting damage of the war. They were films that were intended to be realistic. A key difference between the two films is the fact that Dern's and Voight's characters were both officers, whereas those in *The Deer Hunter* were enlisted men. The next major Vietnam War film to be released in the late 1970s was technically realistic in terms of elements like combat and military equipment, but the story was far more imbued with symbolism than the two previous films.

Francis Ford Coppola's 1979 film *Apocalypse Now* is arguably the most famous film made about the American experience in Vietnam.[18] Loosely based on Joseph Conrad's 1899 novella *Heart of Darkness*, the film depicts a journey undertaken by a character played by Martin Sheen after he is ordered to find and kill a renegade US Army Colonel named Walter Kurtz.[19] Kurtz was played by Marlon Brando, and the cast also featured other performers who enjoyed careers of varying success. Kurtz and Sheen's character, Captain Benjamin Willard, have the most extensive backstories in the film. The enlisted men traveling with Willard come from the typical working-class backgrounds of service personnel shown in other films, and Coppola wisely chose to include a Black soldier played by a young Lawrence Fishburn. Willard successfully completes his mission, although considerable loss of life occurs in the process.

Apocalypse Now is a long film, and Coppola later released a director's cut of it that is even longer.

The most overtly work-related aspect of the various Vietnam War films that were released in the 1970s, beyond the exploitation of everyday Americans who were pressed into military service, was the nature of working in the military. Being in uniform is often presented as being firstly about a person's duty and service to his or her country, with less discussion of what it is like being employed by the military. The films overwhelmingly show a violent male work environment that was bifurcated by rigid organizational hierarchies. Junior officers up to the rank of captain were either depicted sympathetically or as threats to the well-being of the troops they led. Senior officers, perhaps with the exception of John Wayne's Colonel Kirby and Brando's Colonel Kurtz, were distant and often duplicitous bureaucrats. The Vietnam War films of the 1970s did not delve extensively into the post-war working experience of military veterans and their families. Characters who had served in uniform were instead woven into broader theatrical narratives, especially in television.

Cops, Robbers, and Working on the Margins

Crime drama has been a popular film genre since films were first made. Like war films, movies about crime often feature heroes, anti-heroes, and villains. The shift in how crime was shown in film in the 1970s also began with the 1967 film *Bonnie and Clyde*. That film, which starred Warren Beatty and Faye Dunaway, was far more violent than earlier gangster films. It told a stylized tale of the relatively brief careers of 1930s Depression-era criminals Clyde Barrow and Bonnie Parker. Criminals such as Barrow and Parker were alternately admired and feared in American popular culture during the Great Depression, and representations of them on film led viewers to also view them in similar terms. Criminals exuded an allure for many people. There were people, imagined and real, who violated social norms including accepting alienating paid work and instead chose to just steal what they wanted.[20]

A film that markedly changed representations of crime was released in 1972, and it influenced later portrayals of criminal activity.[21] *The Godfather* was also directed by Francis Ford Coppola and was adapted from a 1969 novel of the same title by Mario Puzo.[22] The film showed the rise of the fictional Corleone mafia family, with an emphasis on events in the years immediately following World War II. The cast included younger actors who would later enjoy stellar careers, and one who was already established: Marlon Brando. Brando played family patriarch Vito Corleone. Al Pacino, Talia Shire, James Caan, and Robert Duvall also played key characters, especially Pacino as Michael Corleone.

The film was inspired by actual organized crime activity, but it also had the unintended effect of influencing mafia members who viewed it. *The Godfather* showed crime in organized form, with mafia leaders using managerial structures to run their operations. Organized criminals worked but not in ways that were legal or socially acceptable. The police were the principal opponents of criminals in their various guises, and they could also be anti-heroes even if their work made them part of the coercive arm of the state.[23]

Depictions of police work markedly changed in the 1970s. Prior depictions of law enforcement generally showed clean-shaven white men who closely adhered to the laws they enforced. That portrayal changed in 1971 with the first appearance of Clint Eastwood's character Harry Callaghan. This character lived a solitary existence in San Francisco, generally looked the part of an early 1970s police officer but was prone to bending the rules when pursuing criminals. The villain in the first of the Harry Callaghan films, *Dirty Harry*, was a deranged serial killer who Callaghan eventually kills.[24] That film was followed by the 1973 movie *Magnum Force*, in which the villains were corrupt police officers acting as vigilantes.[25] A third sequel in 1976 called *The Enforcer* involved Callaghan pursuing and killing members of a domestic terrorist organization.[26] The Callaghan character gradually went from principally killing Black criminals in the first film to eventually having a Black man as his partner. There were occupational hazards to being Harry Callaghan's partner as were prone to being killed in the line of duty.

Policing was usually shown to be a dangerous but essential occupation in the 1970s, but at least one film revealed that the police could be corrupt. *Serpico* came out in 1973 and starred Al Pacino as title character.[27] It was based on a book of the same title about former New York City Police Department (NYPD) detective Frank Serpico.[28] The film depicted rampant corruption at basically all levels of the NYPD. The police were shown to be almost as dangerous as the criminals they were supposed to pursue.

Work in law enforcement has typically been a working-class occupation in the United States since Boston created a police force in 1838. This has long put police forces as odds with groups such as striking workers, as a situation exists whereby one part of the working class is restraining or even fighting and killing another section of it. Police work in the 1970s was often portrayed in American films as being dangerous, glamorous, and could also involve operating outside of the boundaries of regular uniformed law enforcement. This was the case with the character John Shaft.[29]

Shaft was the title of a 1971 film starring Richard Rowntree. It was a part of film genre called Blaxploitation and involved a private investigator who works in the Black community. The film became a cultural sensation with its depiction of a smart, savvy man of color prevailing against overwhelming odds. It was an important contribution to the type of actor who was featured in films and also helped alter perceptions of the relationship between Black characters and law enforcement.[30]

Science Fiction: Working in Space

Science fiction became a popular film genre in the four decades following World War II. It had largely been confined to film serials such as *Buck Rogers* and *Flash Gordon* prior to the war, but changes in special effects technology enabled film makers to create visually attractive films with more mature storylines. Science fiction may ostensibly seem about an imagined future, but it is really about examining contemporary issues through a highly imaginative lens. As with other film genres such as war and crime, the changing direction of American science fiction films began in 1968 with Stanley Kubrick's *2001: A Space Odyssey*. That film marked a major evolution in science fiction film making because of the realism of its effects and the complexity of its storyline. Kubrick began making films prior to the director's decade, and he was a major influence on it.[31]

The 1973 film *Westworld* raised questions about uncontrolled technology and pointed toward the problem of what artificial intelligence could do to humanity. The premise of *Westworld* was a theme park populated with life-like androids to which human visitors could do virtually anything they wanted, including killing them. The film starred Yul Brenner as a gunslinging android who shoots human patrons at the park. The android rampage spreads across the western-themed area of the park to other period venues. *Westworld* showed a place that was unlike anything that could be staffed by human workers. The film was also a warning of what artificial intelligence could do if misused.[32]

2001: A Space Odyssey focused on two astronauts and their journey into space with a computer that became sentient. It helped show audiences what could come later, and the next major step in science fiction film evolution arrived in 1977 with George Lucas's *Star Wars*. *Star Wars* was unlike any science film that anyone had previously seen. A combination of remarkable visual and sound effects, and symphonic score, and a quintessential story about good, evil, and redemption made the film into a new type of release: a blockbuster.[33]

What filmgoers did not immediately notice among the visual effects and rousing overall plot was that the characters in *Star Wars*, at least the heroes, had to work their way through space doing whatever they could to earn a living. In contrast, the main villains were in the service of the Empire. Mark Hamill's character Luke Skywalker lived on a desert planet with his aunt and uncle harvesting moisture from the atmosphere.

Harrison Ford's Han Solo piloted a freighter and worked as a smuggler. The economics of fighting the Empire were ubiquitous in the film and its sequels.

The 1970s ended with a science fiction film that showed living and working in space to be boring and routine, while also potentially horrifying. 1979s *Alien* was both science fiction and horror and notably featured a female lead character played by Sigourney Weaver. The premise of a working-class crew on a space freighter coming across an ancient alien civilization, then bringing a seemingly indestructible monster on board managed to include themes about work and even work alienation. The problem of alienation also appeared in films set on 1970s Earth.[34]

Urban Life, Outsiders, and Corporate Power

Shaft was an example of a Black character on the job, but the life of a private investigator came with considerable glamor and danger in his case. The daily reality for most people was much more mundane. Two films from the 1970s showed Black characters at work; one was a comedy and the other dramatic. *Car Wash* came out in 1976, and it featured a predominantly Black cast employed doing minimum wage work at a hand car wash in Los Angeles. It was originally conceived as a musical before being made as a comedy, although the theme song enjoyed considerable radio play.[35]

Car Wash humorously used race and class to show divisions between workers, bosses, customers, and people living in the local neighborhood. It showed the monotony of manual labor and did so in a service sector setting. Characters in the film used a range of strategies to exert some agency on the job, but otherwise felt alienated from their work. *Car Wash* was ultimately a light-hearted film, enjoyed modest box office success, and was even nominated for a Palme D'Or at Cannes. One of the cast members, Richard Pryor, appeared in a 1978 film that had some comedy in it but was otherwise far darker in tone than *Car Wash*.[36]

Labor historians have documented race-based conflict on the job for several decades. Black workers in the United States have long faced barriers to obtaining more skilled and better-paid employment and were often relegated to low-wage and often dangerous work. American unions have made major gains for their members, but they were also run by white men and usually pursued policy agendas that would benefit people like themselves. Women and workers and color had to force their way into the labor movement after World War II.[37]

The 1978 film *Blue Collar* receives little attention in twenty-first-century popular culture and is now principally known by people who have an interest in the labor movement and work-themed films. It is an important representation of industrial workplace conflict made at a time when the post-war economy was shifting against wage workers while the United States was also dealing with the after-effects of the tumultuous 1960s. It featured a large cast including Yaphet Kotto, Richard Pryor, and Harvey Keitel and is a drama about unionized auto workers. *Blue Collar* is a commentary on race, industrial decline, and the impact of corporations on American society. It cost little to make, only $1.7 million, and earned $6.5 million at the box office. This was a respectable return, but not nearly equal to the $307 million earned by the first *Star Wars* film.[38]

Blue Collar was another example of alienation in its different forms appearing on film. It showed workers demonstrating racial animosity and fighting, but it did not show overt mental illness. A 1976 film directed by Martin Scorsese and starring Robert De Niro did show a worker suffering from social alienation and extreme paranoia. De Niro's character, Travis Bickle, was the titular taxi driver living and working in New York City. He is a loner and begins working night shifts as a taxi driver due to insomnia. Bickle tries to befriend a young prostitute, engages in vigilante violence at a brothel, and is heralded as a hero in the press. This was an example of a character who could have been at the Hard Hat Riot in 1970.

Travis Bickle was not a sympathetic anti-hero and *Taxi Driver* later influenced John Hinckley when he attempted to assassinate President Ronald Reagan in 1981.[39] The screenplay for the film was actually based on the diary of Arthur Bremer, who had attempted to assassinate presidential candidate George Wallace in 1972. The film showed another blue-collar worker feeling like a social outsider—Scorcese did not make Bickle a white-collar worker—which in turn helped shape public perceptions about people engaged in work like driving cabs. Referring to an odd perhaps potentially violent social outsider as Travis Bickle became common in popular discourse, much as incidents of workplace violence by postal workers led to the expressing "going postal". Blue-collar workers easily became objects of suspicion.[40]

In contrast to Travis Bickle, New York City architect Paul Kersey engages in a series of vigilante murders in the 1974 film *Death Wish* and is portrayed as a man who suffers a catastrophic personal crisis that leads him to take the law into his own hands. Charles Bronson played Kersey—there would eventually be a series of Death Wish films that deviated from the tone of the first one—and this character also struggles against crime and social decline. Kersey is a white-collar hero while Bickle is a threat.[41]

Corporate management appears in *Blue Collar* and it also appeared in three other notable 1970s films. *Rollerball* was released in 1975 and presented themes of alienation, violence, and corporate domination in a way that continues to be unique. It is close to being a work of science fiction as it is set in a near future where democratic government has disappeared and the world is governed by a handful of corporations that dominate key sectors of the global economy. Professional sports of different types have been displaced by a new game called rollerball which elevates roller derby to new heights of violence. Caan's character is the most famous rollerball player and he gradually rebels against a corporate system that is designed to eventually force him out of the game.[42]

Rollerball is essentially a form of modern Roman gladiatorial game that is meant to distract and control the public. The executives who run the world are mostly faceless, with the exception of John Houseman's character. The film is also somewhat of a commentary on the nature of professional sports in 1970s America as athletes enjoy adulation while playing a game then easily slide into physical degradation and anonymity once they are no longer in it. The lives of the players as workers are closely monitored and they enjoy few real freedoms.

Travis Bickle was an outsider who briefly achieved the notoriety that he sought, but a sequel to *Taxi Driver* may well have shown him descending into further paranoia. In contrast, another 1976 film depicted a down-and-out boxer who became a public hero. *Rocky* was written by Sylvester Stallone, and he played the title character in the film.[43] The viewing public did not realize that it was based on an actual fight that took place in 1975 when then heavyweight champion Muhammad Ali fought an unknown boxer named Chuck Wepner.[44] The Ali-Wepner fight was broadcast on closed-circuit television, whereas other bouts at that time were shown on network broadcasts. Stallone clearly saw the fight.

Rocky Balboa is a club fighter from Philadelphia who personifies the blue-collar American man who could never catch a break. The difference was that a break actually came when Rocky gets the chance to fight fictional heavyweight champion Apollo Creed. Rocky became an aspirational figure for working-class American men—even if Stallone himself had a more affluent upbringing—and the character was resurrected for several sequels in subsequent decades. Rocky lives in a Philadelphia of petty gangsters, meat packing workers, and rundown apartment blocks.

The problem of corporate domination shown in *Rollerball* was satirized in *Network*, which was also released in 1975. It had a large and experienced cast including William Holden and Peter Finch. Finch portrayed a television news anchor who learns that he is going to lose his job due to failing ratings and eventually declares "We're as mad as hell, and we're not going to take this anymore!" on air. *Network* was unlike *Rollerball* as its characters were in white-collar jobs. It showed how even someone in a well-paid professional job with some public notoriety could find themselves facing the same fate as anyone else whose job is eliminated.[45]

There were depictions of workers and the working class during the 1970s that were more light-hearted than the otherwise serious dramas that were often made during the decade. *Saturday Night Fever* was released in 1977 and became known as much for its soundtrack as for its plot. The film focused on the life of Tony Manero, played by John Travolta, and his working-class life in the Bay Ridge neighborhood in Brooklyn. Manero works in a paint store, lives at home with his Italian-American family, and is desperate to experience a more meaningful life. He is the best dancer at a local disco, and eventually takes a step to living and working in Manhattan by the end of the film.[46]

The lives of professional workers did appear on 1970s movie screens, and the 1973 film *The Paperchase* gave viewers some insights into how someone gained professional status in America.[47] It was based on a novel by John Jay Osborn Jr. of the same name.[48] Osborne was a graduate of Harvard Law School and his book was about his experience at that august institution. The film starred Timothy Bottoms, Lindsay Wagoner, and John Houseman. It illustrated the tremendously challenging environment at Harvard Law School, although an enormously lucrative legal career awaited graduates once they graduated.

Saturday Night Fever is a drama with a engaging soundtrack; *Grease* is a musical and it also starred John Travolta. *Grease* was released in 1978, and it helped launch the career of Olivia Newton John. It reflected 1970s nostalgia in American culture and was set in an unidentified large city that was likely meant to be Los Angeles. Travolta plays a high school student named Danny Zuko who meets and falls in love with Newton John's Sandy Olsson. Zuko is a working-class youth enrolled in courses on subjects like automotive repair. 1950s American car culture is woven into the film's plot. The limited work prospects of young working-class Americans are evident behind the film's popular soundtrack.[49]

Unions

Representations of organized labor in American film had largely been negative since Elia Kazan's *On the Waterfront* was released in 1954. Unions were portrayed as corrupt and potentially associated with organized crime, which was a message intertwined with news media messaging about certain unions. The plot in *On the Waterfront* was based on actual events that occurred on the docks in New York City and New Jersey, and the allegations of corruption had been justifiably leveled at the International Brotherhood of Teamsters in the 1950s and 1960s. in the latter case, Teamsters president Jimmy Hoffa was incarcerated in federal prison in 1967 for jury tampering, fraud, and conspiracy. The news media fixed allegations of corruption, which in turn made all unions seem corrupt. The corruption endemic in many corporations was not mentioned.[50]

The United States was home to many different labor organizations in the 1970s, but a few garnered a greater amount of news media attention and that in turn influenced dramatic portrayals of unions. The Teamsters' union was clearly the inspiration for a fictional one called the Federation of Interstate Truckers in Norman Jewison's 1978 film *F.I.S.T.* Sylvester Stallone plays a union president loosely based on Jimmy Hoffa, and the film attempts to show internal union conflict, and the union's involvement with organized crime. The film tried to present a nuanced portrayal of union activity from the New Deal era to the late 1950s but does not always meet that aspiration.

One of the few positive portrayals of unions was released in 1979 when Sally Field portrayed a textile mill worker who organizes her plant in *Norma Rae*. It was yet another film that was based on a actual union organizing led by Crystal Lee Sutton at a mill owned by J.P. Stevens & Company. *Norma Rae* was not marketed as a film about workers' rights and viewers were instead initially led to believe that the film was simply about a woman facing a personal challenge. People learned better when they sat in cinemas and saw the story unfold on screen. Working conditions in the textile mill are abysmal, Norma Rae's father dies on the job after clearly displaying symptoms of a heart attack, and she leads a union organizing drive. The drive succeeds with the help of an organizer from a national union office. *Norma Rae* is one of the few films made in Hollywood in the several decades following World War II that positively portrayed unions and blue-collar working women.[51]

Work and labor appeared in different forms in 1970s Hollywood films. Themes of alienation, race, technological change, corruption, conflict and, in the instance of *Norma Rae*, triumph were all found in films across different genres. The United States experienced major social and economic change during the 1970s, although those changes initially seemed somewhat muted compared to what happened in the preceding decade. The Watergate crisis and resignation of President Richard Nixon, the end of American involvement in Vietnam, the 1973 OPEC oil embargo, and subsequent economic stagflation made Americans feel that the post-World War II economic boom was finally coming to an end. The political right made a step forward with Nixon's first win in the 1968 presidential election and scored a major triumph in 1980 when former Hollywood actor Ronald Reagan defeated incumbent President Jimmy Carter and became America's fortieth president.

The 1980s

The Reagan Decade on Film

Jimmy Carter accomplished much during his four years in office but was stymied by an under-performing economy and a seemingly unsolvable hostage crisis in Iran. He was also prone to perhaps being too honest in his public pronouncements. For example, he went on national television in the summer of 1979 to explain how the United States could get out of its "crisis of confidence". This was not a message that resonated with voters in the following year.[52]

Ronald Reagan presented a very different message about the United States. He was a outwardly a hawskish conservative Republican who had been a two-term governor of California. Reagan still has the unique distinction of being the only American president to have also been president of a union, in his case the presidency of the Screen Actors' Guild from 1947 to 1952 and again from 1959 to 1960. Indeed, Reagan was the second-longest serving president in the guild's history prior to its much later merger with the American Federation of Television and Radio Artists (AFTRA).[53]

Reagan eventually became regarded as anti-union, initially because of the mass firing of striking air traffic controllers in 1981. The early 1980s were also a turning point for American wage workers as incomes significantly failed to keep pace with increases in the cost of living and overall differences between high- and middle-income earners became more pronounced. Wealth accumulation and outright greed began to be admired while corporations became more aggressive toward their workers. The 1970s were a decade driven by new film directors telling realistic stories, but the 1980s were in many ways the Reagan decade on film as who was portrayed on film and how they were depicted changed.

White-Collar Workers

Blue-collar workers like those who were depicted in 1970s films gradually fell to the background in most films made in the 1980s, while white-collar professionals became more prominent. Depictions of women further evolved, as did representations of workers of color. The 1980s were a decade when Americans were willing to address the Vietnam War through movies, such as Oliver Stone's 1986 film *Platoon*, but they otherwise preferred to move on from the types of films made in the 1970s.[54] Critiques of conspicuous consumption appeared in Hollywood films. Oliver Stone began garnering public attention in the 1980s, after the director's decade, but he would have been at home in the 1970s film making milieu. He quickly followed *Platoon* with a film about corporate greed: *Wall Street*.[55] The 1980s were an era when corporate leaders became celebrities. Whereas presidents and chief executive officers were usually stolid figures in gray or black suits into the 1970s, many of them willingly cultivated public profiles in the following decade. A new type of corporate figure—the corporate raider—became prominent in media stories of wealth and power, even if the public did not immediately understand what such a person did for a living.

Stone's 1987 film depicted a Wall Street that was increasingly run by people like Gordon Gekko, played by Michael Douglas. Gekko is a corporate raider who buys distressed companies at a discount, fires the workers, then sells the firm's assets at a profit. He enlists that help of an impressionable junior stockbroker played by Charlie Sheen in schemes to take over the assets of two firms. At one point, Gekko gives a public speech in which he declares "Greed, for lack of a better word, is good". Sheen's character, Bud Fox, cooperates with the US Securities and Exchange Commission to prosecute Gekko for insider trading. Stone crafted a moral tale in *Wall Street* but that aspect of it is often lost on viewers. The Gekko character, while fictional, became a symbol of 1980s excess, and "greed is good" itself became an ethos among people working on Wall Street. The wider message is that it is morally wrong to buy companies, sell their assets, raid their pension plans, and fire all workers did not have the same lasting impact. Michael Douglas did not view Gekko as a heroic character as he agreed in later years to appear in a Federal Bureau of Investigation campaign against insider trading and fraud.[56]

The impact of the 1980s greed ethos on youth was a theme in several films. The 1988 film *Bright Lights, Big City* starred Michael J. Fox. Fox's character works at a magazine, dislikes his job and would rather be a writer, has gone through a divorce, and develops a cocaine addiction. The film is more of a cautionary tale than *Wall Street* as Fox's character, Jamie Conway, eventually loses his job before deciding at the end to turn his life around. There is also no unrepentant character like Gordon Gekko in this film.[57]

Representations of white-collar workers were found in 1980s comedies, with some of them being quite satirical. Michael J. Fox enjoyed considerable box office success at that time and appeared in *The Secret of My Success* in 1987. That film portrayed the almost effortless rise of a young man from a humble background to corporate success. Fox played a somewhat similar character on the television program *Family Ties* and his role in *The Secret of My Success* was doubtless informed by it.[58]

A less well-known satirical comedy called *Head Office* in 1985, and it skewered the nature of managerial work in large corporations. The company that is at the center of the story is simply called INC—meaning incorporated—and the film follows a character played by Judge Reinhold as he is drawn into the firm's corrupt practices. It is an apt description of the type of activity that can occur in corporations, but the film did not do especially well at the box office. The large cast includes Eddie Albert, Jane Seymour, and Danny DeVito.[59]

Every year there are films released that briefly appear in cinemas and disappear in short order. One such 1988 film starred a popular actor—Michael Keaton—and suffered this fate. *Clean and Sober* is a film that accurately depicts substance abuse and the downward spiral of a commercial real estate agent working in Philadelphia. He is accused of being an accessory to the overdose death of a woman with whom he spent the night, and he eventually goes into an addiction treatment program where he encounters other addicts and a counselor played by Morgan Freeman. There is a class-based romantic sub-plot involving Keaton's character and a woman employed in a blue-collar job. This is another film that ends in redemption as Keaton's Daryl Poynter achieves sobriety but loses his job and money.[60]

The idea of addiction to more expensive street drugs like cocaine being linked to white-collar work is a theme that appears in *Clean and Sober* and *Bright Lights, Big City*. White-collar work in 1980s urban environments looks soulless, perhaps depraved, and driven by excess in these films. Lead characters seek and eventually find redemption, but doing so means losing jobs and possible social status. These films also focused on the travails of white men; non-white professionals and women were secondary characters in them. Women did appear in other 1980s films that related to work, and in decidedly mixed depictions.

Women on Film

Women were frequently portrayed in 1980s films in gendered representations of employment, ranging for clerical support to sex work. The directors' decade still had some influence as the 1980s began, and working-class women were still found on film such as the 1983 movie *Silkwood*.[61] That film, starring Meryl Streep, was based on a true story about a whistleblower named Karen Silkwood who was employed at a plant in Oklahoma that fabricated fuel rods for nuclear reactors. It is based on a book called *Who Killed Karen Silkwood?*.[62] The events in the film took place in the early 1970s.

Silkwood lives with her boyfriend and a woman friend—they are all co-workers—and her three children live with her ex-husband. She becomes concerned about safety conditions in the manufacturing facility, is exposed to radiation, and eventually talks to a journalist about lax corporate safety standards. She had become active in her local union soon after being hired at the factory and raised frequent concerns about workplace safety. Silkwood dies in a mysterious car accident, and the argument in the book and film is that she was murdered. The further implication is that the company challenged by Silkwood—Kerr-McGee—was responsible for her death. An actual investigation into the auto accident that caused Silkwood's death concluded that she died in a head-on collision, but investigators also noted that there was unexplained damage to the rear of her car.

Silkwood was directed by Mike Nichols, and it built on themes presented in *Norma Rae*. A working-class woman tries to rely on collective worker action to improve workplace conditions, but in the case of Karen Silkwood, it ends in tragedy rather than triumph. There was also heightened public awareness of workplace safety in the late 1970s and early 1980s, especially when it came to nuclear safety. In 1979, one of the reactors at the Three Mile Island nuclear facility outside Harrisburg, Pennsylvania experienced a partial meltdown. A 1979 film called *The China Syndrome* was based on a fictional near-disaster at a nuclear facility in California and was presciently released mere weeks before the disaster at Three Mile Island actually occurred.[63]

Satire played a role in how female clerical workers were shown on film, and in the example of *9 to 5*, real events informed the film-making process. It starred Lily Tomlin, Jane Fonda, Dolly Parton, and Dabney Coleman in a satirical critique of how women were treated in the late 1970s and early 1980s workplace. Tomlin, Fonda, and Parton all played clerical workers with varying levels of workplace experience, while Coleman portrayed their sexist and unethical boss. Gendered workplace power dynamics are central to the film's plot. The three female lead characters kidnap Coleman and conspire to run the business themselves. *9 to 5* was popular with movie-goers and was helped by an engaging theme song of the same name written and performed by Parton.[64]

9 to 5 was entertaining and empowering for women who watched it, but the film told a tale much smaller in scope than the events that actually inspired it. In the early 1970s, a group of female office workers in Boston began meeting informally to share their workplace grievances. That effort eventually led to the foundation of the 9 to 5 organization, and eventual clerical worker unionization. The 1970s were a period when the impact of second-wave feminism was being felt in the United States. The Equal Rights Amendment, which may yet become part of the US Constitution, was passed by both houses of Congress in 1972. *9 to 5*, as a film, added satire to a much broader narrative about workplace fairness that had been building for many years.[65]

Blue-collar women also advanced themselves on film in the 1980s. The 1983 film *Flashdance* starred Jennifer Beals as a young woman living in Pittsburgh. Her character, Alex Owens, is 18 years old, aspires to be a professional dancer, and is employed in a steel mill. The film ends with her being admitted to a dance conservatory. *Flashdance* received little positive critical attention but earned considerable profit at the box office. It also benefited from having a popular soundtrack.[66]

The office environment was also the setting for the 1988 film *Working Girl* starring Melanie Griffith, Sigourney Weaver, and Harrison Ford.[67]

Griffith's character, Tess McGill, is a working-class woman from Staten Island—a New York City borough—who aspires to be an executive on Wall Street. She instead finds herself working as a secretary for Weaver's character. A romantic sub-plot involving Ford and Griffith soon develops. Tess McGill eventually achieves her career ambition through some subterfuge, and the film ends on a positive note. McGill represents a contemporary female Horatio Alger character, which is popular American cultural archetype.[68] Nobody would want to see a film where someone strives to beat class odds to achieve success and miserably fails.

Women on the job were usually shown doing paid work in 1980s films; unpaid work was less prevalent. Films that focused on the challenges of unpaid domestic work were uncommon on film production rosters, with the exception of the 1983 comedy *Mr. Mom*. Michael Keaton plays a engineer at Ford Motor Company who loses his job. His wife goes back to work and enjoys a career renaissance while Keaton's character Jack Butler stays at home and is quickly overwhelmed with domestic work, especially dealing with the challenges of parenting young children. In that instance, film makers wove a commentary on male, white-collar job loss and deindustrialization into a comedy about gendered career changes.[69]

Class difference and social mobility were found in films about the working lives of women, and two showed women in blue-collar jobs striving for better lives. *An Officer and a Gentleman* starred Richard Gere, Deborah Winger, and Louis Gossette Jr. with Gere portraying aspiring naval aviator Zachary "Zack" Mayo and Winger playing factory worker Paula Pokrifki. Both characters have working-class backgrounds, and both view becoming a Navy officer as a means of achieving upward social mobility. The issue is that Mayo is the one who will have the career, while Pokrifki is essentially relying on him to raise her out of a blue-collar job. He obliges and literally carries her out of her workplace. The ending suggests that a working-class woman needs a man in a white uniform to lift her into middle-class life.

Documentary films rarely achieve the same commercial success and popular attention of dramas, comedies, and other genres but one documentary made in 1976 revealed the lives of women who had spent their lives being union activists. *Union Maids* focused on Kate Hyndman, Stella Nowicki, and Sylvia Woods.[70] It was based on a book by Staughton and Alice Lynd.[71] The film was nominated for an Academy Award for Best Documentary and is a valuable commentary on organizing during the years when industrial unions expanded in the United States.

Youth and Race

1980s youth culture was shaped by class and race but not by the kind of social protest seen in the 1960s. A series of 1980s films by director

John Hughes were full of references to class and gender, although notably not race. His 1985 film *The Breakfast Club* starred Molly Ringwald as Claire Standish, Judd Nelson as John Bender, Anthony Michael Hall as Brian Johnson, Emilio Estevez as Andrew Clark, and Ally Sheedy as Allison Reynolds. The characters are all students sentenced to spend a full day in detention on a Saturday for various infractions, and they all come from differing social-economic backgrounds. Paul Gleason plays Richard Vernon, the vice-principal overseeing the four of them, and John Kapelos is school janitor Carl Reed.[72]

Hughes frequently used the same actors in his films, especially Ringwald, and critics and viewers generally noted his focus on the problems facing young people in their high school years. Class, work, and labor are also seen in Hughes's films. Gleason's vice-principal Vernon clearly no longer has any enthusiasm for his job, while janitor Reed sees the socio-economic dynamics among the students. The principal critique of the Hughes films is that they overwhelmingly feature white characters. The emergence of Spike Lee as a film maker gave audiences much more diverse representations of youth culture in late 1980s America.

Lee acted in as well as directed 1989s *Do The Right Thing*. He played a delivery man named Mookie employed at Sal's Pizzeria, which is owned by Sal played by Danny Aiello. The film is set in the Bedford–Stuyvesant neighborhood in Brooklyn. The area was once predominantly Italian-American when the pizzeria opened and gradually became majority Black. Racial tensions arise in the restaurant and surrounding community, and the film climaxes with Sal's being set on fire by an angry crowd. *Do The Right Thing* was primarily about race in urban America and tensions between different groups, but it was also about work and labor. Lee's Mookie is in a job with no prospects and is employed by a small family business. There are also few good job prospects in the surrounding neighborhood.[73]

Work and Labor Disappears from Science Fiction

Science fiction films changed direction in the 1980s compared with the 1970s as there was a shift more toward fantasy films. Themes of work and labor were largely absent from both fantasy and science fiction, with especially notable exceptions. The third *Star Wars* film was released in 1983, and the *Star Trek* television series returned in a series of films that began in 1979 with *Star Trek: The Motion Picture* and later with *Star Trek II: The Wrath of Khan* in 1982. There were two more *Star Trek* films in the 1980s, and none of them really portrayed work and labor in the same way seen in the *Star Wars* films.

Work and labor appeared in *Star Trek* films to the extent that the characters in them were employed doing something—usually employed as members of Star Fleet or an opposing force—but their living conditions were generally uniform and free from material deprivation. That image reflected the themes that *Star Trek* creator Gene Roddenberry wanted to depict in the original series and films that followed. Roddenberry wanted the environment in which the main characters live, the United Federation of Planets, to be a utopia. He viewed it as a futuristic wagon train to the stars. That view of the future was specific to Roddenberry; other film makers presented a different vision.[74]

Ridley Scott's 1982 film *Blade Runner* was a dystopian tale about a police officer in the future named Rick Deckard whose job is to pursue escaped engineered life forms called replicants.[75] The film was based on Philip K. Dick's 1968 novel *Do Androids Dream of Electric Sheep?*, and Harrison Ford played Deckard.[76] The film was made before the potential to actually clone a living organism had yet been achieved. The human genome was not sequenced until 1990, although the double helix structure of Deoxyribonucleic Acid (DNA) had been discovered in 1953.[77] Androids and other artificial life forms in preceding science fiction films looked mechanical prior to *Blade Runner*, and Ridley Scott took a different direction with them.

Human society shown in *Blade Runner* is technologically advanced, crowded, violent, and grimy. Artificially engineered life forms such as the character Roy Batty played by Rutger Hauer occupied an important social role as they performed jobs that humans did not do, such as military service on other planets and sex work. In fact, they could be designed for different tasks. Replicants were physically stronger and tougher than humans and were provided with fake memories to make themselves believe they were human, but they also had much shorter life spans. A replicant who rebelled would be terminated by a blade runner like Deckard. The film includes a commentary on capitalist behavior as the replicants are created by a firm called Tyrell Corporation.

Blade Runner shared some similarities with *Westworld*. Both films showed artificial intelligence being used to perform tasks that humans could not or would not do. They are both relevant in the third decade of the twenty-first century as it is now entirely plausible to create convincing humanoid artificial intelligence to serve human wants, needs, and desires. Humanity is imperiled in both films by what it has created. *Blade Runner* fared poorly at the box office but became a science fiction classic. Ridley Scott released a director's cut of the film that added greater depth and coherence to it. It raised the possibility that perhaps Deckard himself is a replicant, while further adding poignancy to the film's climax. Roy Batty is a murderous character but is also sympathetic in his quest to live a human life.

Capitalism on Film

American industry and the news media in the 1980s became fixated on the impact that competition with overseas firms had on domestic manufacturing. The relative decline of American automobile firms was often cited as a major socio-economic issue and, as in the case of *Mr. Mom*, found its way into films. Keaton, whether by coincidence or design, also starred in the 1986 film *Gung Ho!* That film, directed by Ron Howard, depicts what happens when a Japanese automaker takes over an American auto assembly plant. Many aspects of Japanese management such as those associated with the Kaizen method and resistance to unions are included in the plot. There is an overall theme that the United States lost its manufacturing edge to Japan and needs to regain it. *Gung Ho* is a comedy that ultimately has a happy ending, although with American auto workers employed in a foreign-owned plant without a union, and with having to adhere to slightly modified Japanese production and management methods. There was a clear message that losing a union in the workplace and submitting to management prerogatives is the price to be paid to hold on to manufacturing jobs and is marked in contrast to the messages conveyed in *Norma Rae*.

One of the last dramas to be made in the 1980s about work and labor went back to the American labor movement's origins. *Matewan* was directed by John Sayles and released in 1987. It is based on events at the Battle of Matewan, which was a coal miners' strike in West Virginia in 1920. There is a long history of conflict between miners and mine owners in Appalachia. The film had an impressive cast including Chris Cooper and James Earl Jones. It had a small production budget but still lost money when released in cinemas. It is considered a classic American labor film and is perennially popular with labor activists, even if it made comparatively little money.[78]

Cooper plays a mine workers' union organizer sent to the town of Matewan to help struggling miners. Themes of class, race, and gender are woven through the film's narrative. The film makers stove to present a realistic portrayal of what working life was like in a coal mining town in 1920s Appalachia, and they largely succeeded. *Matewan* would surely have attracted more public interest had it been released in the late 1970s rather than the end of the Reagan years. It is a film about trying to form unions during a time when organized labor was in significant decline in the United States.

Work and labor issues may have only appeared prominently in a comparatively small number of Hollywood films during the 1980s, but documentary film makers had a history of producing insightful films on the nature of working life in modern America and the decade ended with a 1989 documentary that launched the career of Michael Moore.

Roger & Me revealed the impact of deindustrialization and the policies of General Motors Corporation on Flint, Michigan. Flint is Moore's hometown, and he grew up in an autoworker family.

Roger & Me showed the huge race and class divisions in Flint that existed before and after the decline of General Motors' operations in the city. Footage of holiday celebrations at GM were juxtaposed with seeing a family evicted from their home at Christmas. A woman who supplemented her income farming rabbits showed Moore the process of killing and skinning them. The Michigan bourgeoisie and leadership of GM were either utterly clueless about or completely indifferent to what was happening to the working class. Ronald Reagan left the White House the year before *Roger & Me* was released, and Moore showed much of what Reagan's legacy meant for American wage workers.[79]

From Vietnam to Flint, with Many Points In-between

The work- and labor-themed films of the 1970s and 1980s covered a lot of broad themes. The Vietnam War loomed large in many productions as both main theme and sub-text. The Vietnam films were about loss and possible redemption, with *The Green Berets* and *Rambo* being the sole exceptions. The Vietnam films were often permeated with issues of social class, race, gender difference, and alienation. The Vietnam War film genre presented veterans as damaged either psychologically, physically, or both. The 1988 film *Betrayed* starred Tom Berenger as a Vietnam vet turned violent white supremacist and Deborah Winger as an FBI agent The outraged and potentially dangerous Vietnam veteran became a film stereotype.[80]

Race and class were central to films like *Blue Collar* and *Car Wash*, gender in others like *Norma Rae*, and corporate power was depicted in a range of films from *Rollerball* to *Wall Street*. The treatment of corporate corruption altered as the decades progressed, and audience perceptions also altered over time. Whereas a film like *Silkwood* depicted companies as capable of overt homicidal behavior, Oliver Stone and Michael Douglas inadvertently turned "greed is good" into a 1980s mantra. Many of the films that included depictions of work and labor are included in the US Library of Congress National Film Registry including *Network*, *Union Maids*, *The Godfather*, *Rocky*, *Taxi Driver*, *Saturday Night Fever*, *Norma Rae*, and *Do The Right Thing*. The scenes of working life shown in them are consequently of great enough importance to ensure that they are preserved for posterity.[81]

The political climate change in the United States from the beginning of the 1970s to the end of the 1980s. The film industry and viewing public in the 1980s wanted movies that conveyed more redemptive and uplifting stories than they had seen in the 1970s. People wanted to move on from the upheaval of the late 1960s and earlier 1970s and believe Reagan when he intoned "it is morning again in America" in a 1984 re-election advertisement. This same shift happened in a somewhat similar manner when Americans chose what to watch when they turned on their television sets.[82]

Notes

1 Patterson, John, "Cleopatra, the film that killed-off big-budget epics," 15 July 2013, *The Guardian*, https://www.theguardian.com/film/2013/jul/15/cleopatra-killed-big-budget-epics.
2 Peter Biskind, *Easy Riders, Raging Bulls: How the Sex-Drugs-and-Rock 'n' Roll Generation Saved Hollywood* (New York: Simon and Schuster, 1998), 15.
3 *Easy Rider*, directed by Dennis Hopper (1969; Los Angeles, CA: Pando Company Inc. and Raybert Productions).
4 Jefferson Cowie, *Stayin' Alive: The 1970s and the Last Days of the Working Class* (New York: The New Press, 2010), 355.
5 *The Grapes of Wrath*, directed by John Ford (1940; Los Angeles, CA: Twentieth-Century Fox).
6 *Joe*, directed by John G. Avildsen (1970; Los Angeles, CA: Cannon Group).
7 On the Hard Hat Riot see David Paul Kuhn, *The Hardhat Riot Nixon, New York City, and the Dawn of the White Working-Class Revolution* (Oxford: Oxford University Press, 2020).
8 Thomas Gates, et al., "Report of the President's Commission on an All-Volunteer Armed Force," Washington, DC: 20 February 1970.
9 United States National Archives, "Vietnam War U.S. Military Fatal Casualty Statistics," last reviewed 23 August 2022, https://www.archives.gov/research/military/vietnam-war/casualty-statistics.
10 *M*A*S*H.*, directed by Robert Altman (1970; Los Angeles, CA: Aspen Productions and Ingo Preminger Productions).
11 Richard Hooker, *MASH: A Novel About Three Army Doctors* (New York: William Morrow, 1968).
12 *M*A*S*H.*, developed by Larry Gelbart, 1972–1983, CBS.
13 *The Green Berets*, directed by John Wayne and Ray Kellogg (1968; Los Angeles, CA: Batjac Productions).
14 *The Visitors*, directed by Elia Kazan (1972; Los Angeles: United Artists).
15 *The Deer Hunter*, directed by Michael Cimino (1978; London: EMI).
16 *Coming Home*, directed by Hal Ashby (1978; Los Angeles: Jerome Hellman Productions and Jayne Productions Inc.).
17 Ben Beaumont-Thomas, "Jane Fonda: Hanoi Jane photo was a 'huge mistake,'" 20 January 2015, *The Guardian*, https://www.theguardian.com/film/2015/jan/20/jane-fonda-hanoi-jane-photo-was-a-huge-mistake.
18 *Apocalypse Now*, directed by Francis Ford Coppola (1979; San Francisco: Omni Zoetrope).
19 Joseph Conrad, *Heart of Darkness* (London: Blackwood's Magazine, 1899).
20 *Bonnie and Clyde*, directed by Arthur Penn (1967; Los Angeles, CA: Warner Brothers).
21 *The Godfather*, directed by Francis Ford Coppola (1972; Los Angeles, CA: Paramount Pictures and Alfran Productions).
22 Mario Puzo, *The Godfather* (New York: G.P. Putnam, 1969).

23 Michael Wilson, "With 'The Godfather,' Art Imitated Mafia Life. And Vice Versa," 9 March 2022, *New York Times*, https://www.nytimes.com/2022/03/09/movies/godfather-mafia.html.

24 *Dirty Harry*, directed by Don Siegel (1971; Burbank, CA: The Malpaso Company).

25 *Magnum Force*, directed by Ted Post (1973: Burbank, CA: The Malpaso Company).

26 *The Enforcer*, directed by James Fargo (1976: Burbank, CA: The Malpaso Company).

27 *Serpico*, directed by Sidney Lumet (1973; Los Angeles, CA: Artists Entertainments Complex, Inc. and Produzion De Laurentiis International Manufacturing Company S.P.A.).

28 Peter Maas, *Serpico* (New York: Viking, 1973).

29 Jill Lepore, "The Invention of the Police: Why did American policing get so big, so fast? The answer, mainly, is slavery," 13 July 2020, *The New Yorker*, https://www.newyorker.com/magazine/2020/07/20/the-invention-of-the-police.

30 *Shaft*, directed by Gordon Parks (1971; Los Angeles: Shaft Productions).

31 *2001: A Space Odyssey*, directed by Stanley Kubrick (1968; London: Stanley Kubrick Productions).

32 *Westworld*, directed by Michael Crichton (1973; Los Angeles: Metro-Goldwyn Mayer).

33 *Star Wars*, directed by George Lucas (1977; San Rafael, CA: Lucasfilm).

34 *Alien*, directed by Ridley Scott (1979; Los Angeles, CA: Twentieth-Century Fox and Brandywine Productions)

35 *Car Wash*, directed by Michael Schultz (1976; Los Angeles, CA: Universal Pictures).

36 Festival de Cannes, "Car Wash," accessed 17 November 2023, https://web.archive.org/web/20110924030155/http://www.festivalcannes.com/en/archives/ficheFilm/id/2018/year/1977.html.

37 For example, see Joe William Trotter Jr., *Workers on Arrival: Black Labor in the Making of America* (Berkeley: University of California Press, 2021).

38 *Blue Collar*, directed by Paul Shrader (1978; Los Angeles: Tandem Productions).

39 PBS, "Biography: John Hinckley Jr.," *American Experience*, accessed 17 November 2023, https://web.archive.org/web/20110213093714/https://www.pbs.org/wgbh/americanexperience/features/biography/reagan-hinckley/.

40 *Taxi Driver*, directed by Martin Scorsese (1979; Los Angeles: Bill/Phillips Productions and Italo-Judeo Productions).

41 *Death Wish*, directed by Michael Winner (1974; Los Angeles, CA: Dino Di Laurentis Corporation).

42 *Rollerball*, directed by Norman Jewison (1975; London: Algonquin Films).

43 *Rocky*, directed by John G. Avildsen (1976; Los Angeles, CA: Chartoff-Winkler Productions).

44 Eric Raskin, "'Real Rocky' Wepner finally getting due," 25 October 2011, *ESPN*, https://www.espn.com/boxing/story/_/page/IamChuckWepner/chuck-wepner-recognized-rocky-fame.

45 *Network*, directed by Sidney Lumet (1976; Los Angeles: Metro-Goldwyn Mayer).

46 *Saturday Night Fever*, directed by John Badham (1977; London: Robert Stigwood Organization).

47 James Bridges, director, *The Paperchase* (1973; Los Angeles: Rodrick Paul and Robert C. Thompson).

48 John Jay Osborn, Jr., *The Paperchase* (New York: Houghton-Mifflin, 1971).
49 *Grease*, directed by Randal Kleiser (1978; Los Angeles, CA: Allan Carr Enterprises and Stigwood Group).
50 For an account of the events that shaped the making of *On the Waterfront* see James T. Fisher, *On the Irish Waterfront: The Crusader, the Movie, and the Soul of the Port of New York* (Ithaca: Cornell University Press, 2010).
51 *Norma Rae*, directed by Martin Ritt (1979; Los Angeles, CA: Twentieth-Century Fox).
52 Jimmy Carter, "Crisis of Confidence," 15 July 1979, PBS American Experience, https://www.pbs.org/wgbh/americanexperience/features/carter-crisis/.
53 SAG-AFTRA, "SAG presidents," accessed 17 November 2023, https://www.sagaftra.org/about/our-history/sag-presidents.
54 *Platoon*, directed by Oliver Stone (1986; Los Angeles, CA: Orion Pictures).
55 *Wall Street*, directed by Oliver Stone (1987; Los Angeles, CA: American Entertainment Partners and Amercent Films).
56 Jason Rodriguez, "Michael Douglas, aka Gordon Gekko, recants: greed is not good," 28 February 2012, *The Guardian*, https://www.theguardian.com/film/from-the-archive-blog/2012/feb/28/fbi-michael-douglas-wall-street.
57 *Bright Lights, Big City*, directed by James Bridges (1988; Los Angeles, CA: Mirage).
58 *The Secret of My Success*, directed by Herbert Ross (1987; Los Angeles, CA: Rastar).
59 *Head Office*, directed by Ken Finkleman (1985; Los Angeles, CA: HBO Pictures and Silver Screen Partners).
60 *Clean and Sober*, directed by Glenn Cordon Caron (1988; Los Angeles, CA: Imagine Entertainment).
61 *Silkwood*, directed by Mike Nichols (1983; Los Angeles, CA: ABC Motion Pictures).
62 Howard Kohn, *Who Killed Karen Silkwood* (New York: Summit Books, 1981).
63 *The China Syndrome*, directed by James Bridges (1979; Los Angeles, CA: IPC Films and Major Studio Partners).
64 *9 to 5*, directed by Colin Higgins (1980; Los Angeles, CA: IPC Films).
65 On the 9 to 5 movement and the movie it inspired see Ellen Cassidy, *Working 9 to 5: A Women's Movement, A Labor Union, and the Iconic Movie* (Chicago: Chicago Review Press, 2022).
66 *Flashdancce*, directed by Adrian Lyne (1983; Los Angeles: PolyGram Pictures).
67 *Working Girl*, directed by Mike Nichols (1988; Los Angeles, CA: Twentieth-Century Fox).
68 Horatio Alger was a nineteenth-century American author who wrote fictional novels about young men from poor backgrounds who raised themselves up the socio-economic hierarchy. For an example see Horatio Alger, *Ragged Dick; or, Street Life in New York with the Boot Blacks* (New York: A.K. Loring, 1868).
69 *Mr. Mom*, directed by Stan Dragoti (1983; Los Angeles, CA: Sherwood Productions).
70 *Union Maids*, directed by Jim Klein, Julia Reichert, and Miles Mogulescu (1976; Newburgh, NY: New Day Films).
71 Staughton Lynd and Alice Lynd, *Rank and File: Personal Histories of Working-Class Organizers* (Boston: Beacon Press, 1973).
72 *The Breakfast Club*, directed by John Hughes (1985; Los Angeles, CA: A&M Films and Channel Productions).

73 *Do The Right Thing,* directed by Spike Lee (1989; New York, NY: Forty Acres and a Mule Filmworks).
74 Richard Zogolin, "A Bold Vision: How Star Trek First Made It to the Screen," 21 July 2016, *Time,* https://time.com/4406710/star-trek-history-excerpt/.
75 *Blade Runner,* directed by Ridley Scott (1982; Los Angeles CA and Hong Kong: The Ladd Company, Shaw Brothers, Blade Runner Partnership).
76 Philip K. Dick, *Do Androids Dream of Electric Sheep?* (New York: Doubleday, 1968).
77 National Institutes of Health, "The Discovery of the Double Helix, 1951-1953," accessed 17 November 2023, https://profiles.nlm.nih.gov/spotlight/sc/feature/doublehelix and National Institutes of Health, "The Human Genome Project," accessed 17 November 2023, https://www.genome.gov/human-genome-project.
78 *Matewan,* directed by John Sayles (1987; New York, NY: Cinecom).
79 *Roger & Me,* directed by Michael Moore (1989; Los Angeles, CA: Dog Eat Dog Films).
80 *Betrayed,* directed by Costa-Gravas (1988; Los Angeles, CA: CST Telecommunications Co., Winkler Films, and United Artists). On the Vietnam War's legacy in the United States, including in popular culture, see Gordon Arnold, *The Afterlife of America's War in Vietnam* (Jefferson, NC: McFarland & Company, 2006).
81 Library of Congress, "Complete National Film Registry Listing," accessed 17 November 2023, https://www.loc.gov/programs/national-film-preservation-board/film-registry/complete-national-film-registry-listing/.
82 Gil Troy, *Morning in America: How Ronald Reagan Invented the 1980s* (Princeton: Princeton University Press, 2007), 296.

2 Television

Television was the most popular entertainment medium in the 1970s and 1980s, especially in the first decade. Widespread use of video cassette recorders and early pay-per-view channels altered consumer viewing habits in the second decade, but network programming was still dominant even with those changes in technology. Work and labor appeared frequently in 1970s and 1980s television programs, but in a different way than in film. The 1970s were not so much a director's decade as more of a producer's decade due to the way that television programs were developed in contrast with films. Television in the 1970s and 1980s showed working life in a way that was not always apparent on film. They were decades when viewers could switch on their televisions and see something of their own working lives, as television reflected changing socio-economic and political trends happening in the United States.

The 1970s

Norman Lear's Working People

The working-class family had been common on network television since networks began widespread broadcasting in the 1950s. Working families were shown in program like the *Honeymooners* and that trend continued in the early 1970s with a program that led to major spinoff series. The representations of working life that Americans saw on their TV screens in the 1970s were significantly shaped by one producer: Norman Lear. Lear grew up in a lower-middle-class household, served in the US Army Air Force in World War II, and traveled to Los Angeles after the war and began working in Hollywood. By the end of the 1960s, he had sufficient experience and influence in film and television production to successfully create a new situation comedy about a blue-collar family. *All in the Family* starred Carroll O'Connor as Archie Bunker, Jean Stapleton as his wife Edith, Sally Struthers as

DOI: 10.4324/9781003384564-3

daughter Gloria, and Rob Reiner as son-in-law Michael.[1] It was based on a British program called *Till Death Do Us Part* and was for a time the most popular show on television. The Bunkers lived in Queen's, which was then a white working-class borough in New York City. Archie was a World War II veteran who worked as a loading dock foreman, while also supplementing his income by working as a taxi driver at night. O'Connor was not at all like Archie Bunker, but the character became a cultural icon. Archie's wing chair and Edith's armchair are now on display at the Smithsonian's National Museum of American History.[2]

Contemporary political and social issues were always part of *All in the Family* scripts in a way that they would never be in later sitcoms. Race, gender, class, and the generational divide between the World War II generation and their Baby Boomer children were on full display every week. This aspect of the show led to spinoffs, and those subsequent shows brought characters into living rooms that were unlike anything that average Americans had seen before on screen. For instance, changes in the social role of women and how they viewed themselves were depicted in *Maude*. That sitcom was named for Edith Bunker's cousin Maude Findlay, with the character played by Beatrice Arthur. Maude was liberal while Archive Bunker was conservative, and the two humorously clashed when Maude appeared as a guest character on *All in the Family*. She was wealthy, married four times, and her single daughter and grandson lived with her. Maude embodied much of what white working-class men disliked about the direction that America took in the 1970s.[3]

Norman Lear and CBS, the network on which *All in the Family* was broadcast, followed Maude with depictions of Black families in 1970s America. *The Jeffersons* was a direct spinoff of *All in the Family* and featured George and Louise Jefferson, played by Sherman Helmsley and Isabel Sanford. The link to the earlier series was Jefferson's son Lamont, played by Michael Jonas Evans, who was friends with Michael and Gloria Stivic. The Jeffersons were also neighbors with the Bunkers in Queens before moving to Manhattan, with that move made possible through the success of George's dry-cleaning business.[4]

The Jeffersons had a multi-racial cast—including characters in an inter-racial marriage—and it depicted an upwardly mobile, middle-class, self-employed businessman interacting with other people like him. This was a type of character that had not previously been shown weekly on American sitcoms. Norman Lear was visited by three members of the Black Panthers party who were fans of his shows but wanted to see Black characters actually succeeding and doing well economically. *The Jeffersons* ran for ten years, although ended abruptly in 1985. The show that the Black Panthers who visited Lear had in mind was another spinoff, this time from *Maude* rather than directly from *All in the Family*.[5]

Good Times premiered in 1974, a year before *The Jeffersons*. It starred John Amos and Esther Rolle as James and Florida Evans, and their three children. The family is shown living in a housing project in Chicago. One son, J.J., was played by Jimmie Walker. James works a variety of jobs, Florida as a maid, and the family clearly lives from payday to payday. *Good Times* humorously addressed racial and economic inequality, urban violence, and a range of other issues. It ran for six years and was popular with viewing audiences. It was produced by Norman Lear, but crucially created by two Black men: Michael Jonas Evans and Eric Monte. It was not a white person's view of Black life in America, but rather a Black view of life in America being shown to white audiences. *Good Times* showed Black people doing many different jobs to get by, while hoping for better prospects for their children.[6]

The problem of being poor and just getting by was also on display in *Sanford and Son*.[7] Norman Lear was an uncredited producer of that sitcom, and it was based on a British program called *Steptoe and Son*.[8] *Sanford and Son* starred Red Foxx as junk dealer Fred Sanford, with Desmond Wilson as his son Lamont. Fred lived in the Watts area of Los Angeles. Foxx was a well-established comedian by the time he was chosen to play Fred Sanford and the show invariably focused on Fred's schemes, disagreements with Lamont, and disputes with his late wife's sister with considerable humor involved in the narrative. *Sanford and Son* provided American households with yet another series that showed them Black actors and characters in a way that they had not previously experienced.[9]

There were TV shows that looked like they were created by Norman Lear that were created by other producers. *Chico and the Man* was created by James Komack and aired on NBC from 1974 to 1978. It starred Jack Albertson as Ed Brown and Freddie Prinze as Chico Rodriguez and was about a garage owner who hires a young Mexican man. The show used cultural differences between Albertson and Rodriquez for humorous plots and was popular from the time it premiered. The show came to an end because of Prinze's untimely death in 1977.[10]

Bonded Labor on Screen

American television was replete with period shows from the 1950s onward, and they were often westerns. *Gunsmoke*, starring James Arness, ran from 1955 to 1975 and it was joined by other shows like *The Big Valley* and *Bonanza*. Such programs often depicted an idealized account of America's past, and they usually had overwhelming white casts with an occasional non-white actor appearing in supporting or guest roles. The fact that enslaved labor occupied a prominent place in

America's past was ignored until 1977 when Alex Haley's book *Roots* was adapted into a mini-series of the same name.

Haley was a journalist who grew up in a middle-class Black family in Ithaca, New York, served in the US Coast Guard in World War II, and developed a talent for writing. His work appeared in prominent magazines, and he gained public attention for writing *The Autobiography of Malcolm X*. Haley agreed to ghost-write it.[11] Malcom X was a prominent civil rights leader but getting him to actually speak about his own life rather than his political positions initially proved difficult for Haley. He was ultimately successful, and *The Autobiography of Malcolm X* became a bestseller. Haley then followed it with *Roots*, which he based on his own family's history.[12] Critics of the book said that there were aspects of it that were factually incorrect, but that did not prevent it from being a bestseller.

Haley traced the journey of his ancestor Kunta Kinte, a Mandinka man living along the River Gambia in West Africa, into slavery in Virginia. The book ended in contemporary America. It shot to the top of bestseller lists and ABC turned it into a mini-series the following year. That mini-series was also enormously popular and won several awards. Haley may have engaged in some creative license with his book, but that did neither prevent it nor the mini-series from at times shocking white America. The mini-series naturally had a large Black cast, including actors like LeVar Burton, and it looked to be a turning point for Black actors in Hollywood. The 1977 mini-series was followed by another one in 1979, with the first mini-series covering the period up to the end of the US Civil War and the second one the period up to Haley's lifetime.[13]

When Americans saw the lives of enslaved people shown in *Roots* they saw practices and treatment of other human beings that was horrific. They were also seeing the importance of bonded labor in America from the early eighteenth century to the end of the Civil War. No Hollywood production has yet to adequately depict the meaning and legacy of enslavement in the United States, but *Roots* certainly started the process. The way in which the use of enslaved labor shaped the relationship between labor and capital across the country has yet to properly appear in either film or television. For a country that was used to seeing depictions of slavery through films like *Gone with the Wind*, *Roots* was an entirely new viewing experience.[14]

Cops and Robbers

Crime dramas were an established staple of American television by 1970, and they continued to be as the decade progressed while also evolving. Police dramas did not integrate the gritty depictions of crime that were appearing on film. For example, *Adam 12* premiered in 1968 and ran until 1975. Its principal stars were Kent McCord as Officer Jim Reed and Martin Milner as Officer Joseph "Pete" Malloy. *Adam 12* was supposed to be based on actual Los Angeles Police Department cases and procedures, but much of the criminal activity shown in it was benign compared with what appeared in films made during the early 1970s. Problems such as petty theft, robbery, and occasional violent crime comprised *Adam 12*'s plots. The police were shown receiving respect from everyday citizens, and police operated within the rules unlike those shown in *Serpico*. The police in *Adam 12* were honest, hard-working, and not beset with emotional problems or prone to violence because of their work.[15]

Police work was increasingly portrayed on TV screens as it was being shown in movies. There was nothing quite like a TV equivalent of Harry Callahan, but programs were made to appeal to a younger and more diverse demographic. *Hawaii Five-0* starring Jack Lord and a diverse cast of actors premiered in 1968 and ran until 1980.[16] The exotic locale in which the show was set attracted viewers, as did the theme song written by Morton Stevens. *Hawaii Five-0* glamorized police work. A less exotic local that Honolulu—Los Angeles—was the setting for *Emergency*. Its principal stars were Randolph Mantooth as Johnny Gage and Kevin Tighe as Roy DeSoto. The show focused on the lives and work of young fire and paramedic crews, made emergency response work seem exciting, and was intended to attract younger viewers.[17] Southern California was also the setting for the popular police action series *Starsky and Hutch* that starred David Soul and Paul Michael Glaser, and ran from 1975 to 1979.[18] The red 1976 Ford Grand Torino in that show was as much one of its stars as Soul and Glaser.

Humor was occasionally used to depict police work, and *Barney Miller* was a leading example of that type of portrayal. It starred Hal Linden as the eponymous character, and he was also joined by a diverse if overwhelming male cast. Viewers saw an often eccentric cast of supporting actors come across the *Barney Miller* set every week. Police work was shown as ironic and even entertaining in this show. It was also unique as it was set entirely in a police station with characters rarely shown outside of that environment.[19]

The South

The working-class anti-hero was featured on television along with film portrayals in the 1970s, and this type of character was quite prominent in the *Dukes of Hazard*. That show ran from 1979 to 1985 and was part of a television and film sub-genre that depicted characters living and unofficially working in the American South. The 1977 film *Smoky and the Bandit* was a cinematic example of this sub-genre. The *Dukes of*

Hazard was about Bo and Luke Duke, young men living in Hazard County, Georgia where they previously worked running moonshine. They were played by John Schneider and Tom Wopat. They were joined by their Uncle Jessie, played by Denver Pyle, and their cousin Daisy who was played by Catherine Bach.[20]

The Dukes never appeared to have legitimate jobs, yet were described as two "modern day Robin Hoods" in the show's theme song. They faced-off against local crooked businessman Boss Hogg, portrayed by Sorrell Book and Sherriff Roscoe P. Coltrane played by James Best. The *Dukes of Hazard* depicted the American South as corrupt and somewhat lawless because the police were incompetent, with good old boys like the Dukes taking affairs into their own hands. It was also a popular series that was not set in a northern state or in the west. It glorified rural, southern, blue-collar working life. The show's popularity was such that a similar show called *B.J. and the Bear* starring Greg Evigan and a chimpanzee was produced. The premise in that instance was a truck driver traveling across the country solving problems, dealing with criminals of varying types, and otherwise acting as yet another benevolent anti-hero.[21]

The *Dukes of Hazzard* presented highly gendered representations of working people, even if their work was illegal. The women were usually scantily clad and, with the exception of Daisy, in need of male protection. The shows included some violence but nothing especially gratuitous. It was overwhelmingly white and did not include any major non-white characters, which is telling considering that Georgia has large Black population. The fact that the show also featured the Dukes racing around in a 1969 Dodge Charger with a Confederate flag emblazoned across the roof surely did not endear it to non-white audiences.

Women on the Job

The impact of second-wave feminism was evident in television shows other than the *Dukes of Hazzard*. No program better exemplified that trend than the *Mary Tyler Moore* show. The show was named for Mary Tyler Moore, who had first come across television screens as Laura Petrie on the *Dick Van Dyke Show*. Moore was a middle-class housewife in the *Dick Van Dyke* show, which ran from 1961 to 1966, but a single professional woman in her eponymous 1970s program. Her character, Mary Richards, was a producer working at a local TV station in Minneapolis.[22]

The cast of the *Mary Tyler Moore Show* cast included Ed Asner, Gavin McLeod, Ted Knight, Betty White, Cloris Leachman, and Valerie Harper. The storylines were always humorous but also included serious themes related to gender and class. Asner's Lou Grant was gruff and not always ready to accept a working woman like Richards. Knight's Ted Baxter personified the type of character that Americans expected to see when turning on a local news broadcast.[23]

The *Mary Tyler Moore Show* presented an image of femininity that was different from what was usually presented on American television, and Moore's character was frequently pushing against established American social norms through her interaction with the other characters on the show. Moore's Mary lived on her own in an apartment, earned a reasonable living, and exhibited progressive social views. In contrast, Asner's Lou was secretly progressive under his gruff exterior. Mary Tyler Moore clearly wanted to show, through her own production company, a modern portrayal of American women in the 1970s that was liberated from how they had usually been portrayed in film and television.

Work and labor themes appeared in episodes of the show. For example, a 1971 episode revolved around a writers' strike. Lou and Mary were compelled to cover work normally done by unionized workers at the television station, and Mary had to reluctantly cross a picket line. This is a theme that would be hard to find on a television show in the third decade of the twenty-first century. Other episodes included issues such as how much money people were earning and how it impacted their living standards.[24]

The *Mary Tyler Moore Show* enjoyed sufficient popularity to inspire the development of three spinoff shows: *Lou Grant*, *Rhoda*, and *Phyllis*. The first was more dramatic than comedic, and again starred Ed Asner as Grant. *Rhoda* starred Valerie Harper as Mary Richards's best friend.[25] *Phyllis* starred Cloris Leachman as Phyllis Lindstrom, who had had been Richards' landlord and friend on *The Mary Tyler Moore Show*.[26] Work themes were less overtly present in *Rhoda* and *Phyllis* than on *The Mary Tyler Moore Show* but are still evident. Both Rhoda and Phyllis worked at low-paid service sector jobs. Phyllis had been married to a rich physician and had to try to re-enter the workforce, while also moving in with her mother out of financial necessity. Rhoda married during the series, and later divorced, but both *Rhoda* and *Phyllis* reflected working experiences that were different than those experienced by Mary Richards.

Lou Grant was primarily a drama with occasional comedy included, and Ed Asner reprised his *Mary Tyler Moore Show* character in the title role. Its creators sought to depict the reality of working in the newsroom of a daily paper. One of its episodes focused on a strike, and it actually showed the tensions that can arise between labor and management when a work stoppage happens.[27]

Women living and working on the economic margins was a theme found on other television shows, and *One Day at a Time* was one of them. That sitcom starred Bonnie Franklin as Ann Romano, a single mother living in an apartment in Indianapolis with her two daughters. The complex domestic relations of divorced and single-parent households are central to the weekly plotlines of *One Day at a Time*, but work and labor themes are also woven into storylines. Ann has a career and starts a business with another woman but also faces economic challenges raising two teenage daughters, who were played by Valerie Bertinelli and Mackenzie Phillips. The daughters, Julie and Barbara, complete high school and move into the labor force.[28]

The theme of women having to take low-paid work out of necessity was also found in *Alice*, starring Linda Lavin. That sitcom from 1976 to 1985 and depicted a recently widowed single mother who took a job waitressing at a diner in Phoenix while first attempting to travel to Los Angeles from New Jersey. The cast included waitress Florence Castleberry played by Polly Holliday, Vera Gorman played by Beth Howland, and diner owner Mel Sharples played by Vic Tayback. *Alice* was principally set in the diner owned by Mel, and its humor did not always put a positive veneer over the difficult circumstances of Alice's life. She lived in a one-bedroom apartment with her son. Vic and Vera each had even smaller apartments, while Florence lived in a trailer. Alice was compelled to take a waitressing job even though she dreamed of pursuing a singing career. All of the characters on *Alice* were barely getting by financially.[29]

Work and Nostalgia

Nostalgia became a more prominent part of American popular culture than it had been in previous decades. Interest in what seemed like simpler times, specifically the 1950s, was shaped by dissatisfaction with the direction of the United States in the 1970s and what had occurred in the 1960s. George Lucas's 1973 film *American Graffiti* started this trend, and it was accelerated by the creation of the sitcom *Happy Days* in 1974. That series starred Ron Howard, who had also been in *American Graffiti*, along with Henry Winkler and several other supporting characters. Howard played Ritchie Cunningham, Winkler was Arthur "Fonzie" Fonzarelli and the show was set in Milwaukee.[30]

Working themes were prevalent throughout *Happy Days* during its ten-year run on network television, and it was set in a period from the mid-1950s to the mid-1960s. The characters were mostly working class from Fonzie as a motorcycle riding, leather jacket-wearing tough guy to Arnold, who operated the diner that teenage Ritchie and his friends frequented. The lives of working people were generally shown to be positive, which was consistent with the name of the show. There were difficult themes covered in *Happy Days*, but it mainly celebrated a period when the United

States was prosperous and had yet to contend with the full impact of the Vietnam War. *Happy Days* was yet another show that led to spinoffs: *Laverne and Shirley, Mork and Mindy,* and *Joanie Loves Chachi.* The latter two shows had few references to work and labor.

Laverne and Shirley was about the lives of two women working in the fictional Shotz brewery: Laverne DeFazio played by Penny Marshall, and Shirley Feeney played by Cindy Williams.[31] The characters were opposites in terms of personality, and the weekly plots revolved around their working and personal lives. *Laverne and Shirley* showed empowered working-class women earning their own money. Women with similar lives in 1970s America would have undoubtedly watched it and been reminded of their own lives and co-workers when they looked at Laverne DeFazio and Shirley Feeney. This was also a program that drew somewhat from *The Odd Couple,* which was another 1970s series starring Jack Klugman and Tony Randall as male room mates who were polar opposites in terms of personality.[32] That show was also adapted from an earlier film. The other two *Happy Days* spinoffs included fewer work and labor themes but that collection of shows, along with the various Norman Lear productions, reflected the success of spinoff programming in the 1970s.

The nostalgia theme was also fully integrated into *The Waltons.*[33] This drama was set in a Depression-era county in Virginia and revolved around the eponymous Walton family. It first aired as a television movie called *The Homecoming: A Christmas Story,* and CBS ordered a season of episodes based on the success of that film.[34] *The Waltons* was often viewed as wholesome television. The weekly plotlines focused on working and living in a rural setting. A lot of unpaid domestic work with highly gendered divisions of labor were shown, and the general difficulty of finding paid work during the Depression was a theme. The time period covered during the show's run from 1972 to 1981 focused on the years from 1933 to 1946, which included World War II. All four of the Walton boys serve in the military during the war years. The cast of *The Waltons* was multi-generational, with parents John and Olivia presiding over a household that included his parents and seven children. The oldest son, John-Boy, became somewhat of a cultural icon as each episode concluded with family members retiring for the evening and different characters calling out "goodnight, John-Boy". Ralph Waite and Michael Learned played John and Olivia, and Richard Thomas was John-Boy.

The Waltons showed a Depression-era America that TV viewers wanted to see. It rarely showed any racial diversity among the cast of supporting actors. It was like a Norman Rockwell painting come to life, and it was popular with weekly television viewers. It showed the Walton family dealing with difficult events, such as the death of Grandpa Zebulon Walton actor Will Geer and a stroke suffered by Grandma Esther Walton actor Ellen Corby, and those events elicited sympathy from viewers and made the family seem familiar. The show showed a family dealing with financial hardship, but not on the scale of the families depicted in *The Grapes of Wrath* or in the photographs of Dorothea Lang. It was a vision of being part of the white rural working class that did not cause people to feel conflicted or outraged.[35]

A similar approach to depicting work and family life was seen in *Little House on the Prairie*, which ran from 1974 to 1983, and was based on a series of books by Laura Ingalls Wilder and depicted life in a prairie household in the 1870s. It was somewhat like an 1870s version of *The Waltons*. Work was a constant theme in *Little House on the Prairie*, and both paid and unpaid work was continual for settlers on the American prairies. The image of rural 1870s Americana depicted in *Little House on the Prairie* tended to be pastoralized even though everyday aspects of life at that time shown in it were correct. Characters contracted life-threatening bouts of illnesses that became easily treated in the twentieth century, Mellissa Sue Anderson's character Mary Ingalls permanently lost her sight, and people died in different episodes. Michael Landon was the show's star and one of its executive producers. He had prime-time television experience having previously starred in the western drama *Bonanza*, which was produced from 1959 to 1973. Landon knew what American viewers wanted to see when they were presented with TV depictions of life in the late 1800s American West, and he and the other people on the show provided it.[36]

Teachers and DJs

Hollywood periodically shows interest in drama and comedy that can be depicted within a school setting. Youth culture was part of programs like *Happy Days* and was particularly the focus of *Welcome Back Kotter*. It ran from 1975 to 1979 and starred Gabe Kaplan as high school remedial studies teacher Gabe Kotter. The school is the fictional James Buchanan High School in Bensonhurst, which is part of Brooklyn. Kotter is himself revealed to be a graduate of the school.[37]

The students in *Welcome Back Kotter* were a group of young men who were called the Sweathogs, such was their level of incorrigibility. The cast was racially and ethnically diverse and included John Travolta as Vinny Barbarino. The show drew an affectionate following because it was funny, but also because of the nature of the characters themselves. Kotter could have been portrayed as some kind of educational crusader but instead came across as an advocate and supporter for the students. The students reciprocated by more or less paying attention.

The work environment in *Welcome Back Kotter* was somewhat mirrored in *The White Shadow* starring Ken Howard. Howard played Ken Reeves, a former professional basketball player who moves to

Los Angeles to become a coach at a tough Los Angeles high school. The players are all men from racially and ethnically diverse backgrounds, although from poor and working-class families. There was some humor in *The White Shadow,* but it was mainly a drama that depicted the challenges of working in a high school populated with young people with few immediate life prospects. Teaching and coaching are shown to be demanding in the show, with the reward of helping people being more compensation than actual salary.[38]

Youth culture was part of shows like *Welcome Back Kotter* and *The White Shadow* and it was a related aspect of sitcom *WKRP in Cincinnati. WKRP* was set in a fictional AM radio station at a time when AM radio was still popular and a key part of youth culture. *WKRP* was not depicted as huge and dominant, but as a local radio station that was owned by an eccentric boss and staffed by an equally eccentric group of workers. It included Gary Sandy as station manager Andy Travis, Gordon Jump as station owner Arthur Carlson, Frank Bonner as sales representative Herb Tarlek, Loni Anderson as secretary Jennifer Marlowe, Tim Reid as disc jockey Venus Flytrap, Jan Smithers as reporter Bailey Quarters, Richard Sanders as reporter Les Nessman, and Howard Hesseman disc jockey Johnny Fever.[39]

The workers shown in WKRP mostly hoped to be doing something better later in the careers, or they accepted that they had landed in the best positions they would find. Some, like Les Nessman, showed great enthusiasm for their work. The Nessman character is perhaps the only one in American television history to show such a desire to have his own office that he demarcated walls and a door on the floor with packing tape. Carlson is an inept if kindly owner, while Travis essentially runs the station. The show occasionally dealt with serious topics, but the emphasis was firstly on often sophisticated humor.

American Soap Operas and Not Working

This narrative has not been comparative thus far, but there is one aspect of American television programming before, during, and after the 1970s that warrants a brief comparison with programming in other countries: the soap opera. This TV format appeared in the United States in 1949 with the premiere of *These Are My Children.*[40] It was followed by several others in subsequent decades including *All My Children, As the World Turns,* and *Another World.*[41] Soaps, as they were colloquially called, were broadcast during afternoons when women at home doing domestic work could watch them. The unpaid domestic worker was consequently viewed as a lucrative viewing audience, even though the value of women's work was scarcely recognized and instead taken as a given part of family life.

One of the main details of American soaps was that few of the characters actually seemed to work despite generally enjoying at least middle-class standards of living. This was a major contrast with an overseas soap like the UK's *Coronation Street*, which has now been on air for 63 years. Characters in *Coronation Street* all work, and the vast majority are in working-class occupations such as tradesperson or bar keeper. *Coronation Street* is broadcast in the evening and is intended for a wider viewing audience than an American soap. Large swathes of the American TV audience— overwhelmingly men—may never have seen a soap unless they had a day off work. There were occasional exceptions to the pattern of work being largely absent from soaps, such as medical dramas, but a middle to upper-middle-class lifestyle seemingly devoid of daily labor otherwise predominated in soap storylines. Soap operas were supposed to be escapist, and escapism included seeing wealthy people doing relatively little to earn a living and instead spend their time in a series of complicated romantic entanglements. They were also crafted to draw viewers into long, constantly evolving plots that spanned not just one season but perhaps several. This was a significant contrast with TV sitcoms and dramas that usually presented stories devoted to single episodes.[42]

The 1980s

Professional Workers

The decade of economic stagnation and crisis that influenced television programming in the United States in the 1970s quickly gave way to images and stories of a country that reflected the social and cultural shift that happened in the Reagan era. Ronald Reagan received a generally positive reception in Hollywood, because even though he had moved rightward down the political spectrum since his years as Screen Actors' Guild president, he was still regarded by Hollywood as one their own. Actors such as Clint Eastwood were guests at White House events. When asked about being president, Reagan himself once said he "wondered how you could do the job if you hadn't been an actor".[43]

Professional and managerial workers, especially the former, were found in the medical drama *St. Elsewhere* that ran from 1982 to 1988. It was set in the fictional Boston hospital called St. Eligius, and its large ensemble cast included Denzel Washington and Howie Mandel. It was supposed to show the nature of actually working in medicine, and it largely succeeded. Medical dramas had been on TV screens for many years, but *St. Elsewhere* was meant to be more realistic than previous shows and it mainly succeeded. It showed the nature of medical training, the self-doubts that medical practitioners could face, tension between medical personnel and hospital administrators, race, gender, and class. Episodes often included subplots that revolved around moral dilemmas that arose in medicine.[44]

Medical dramas continued to be a staple of US television beyond the 1980s, and they have been closely followed by legal dramas. *L.A. Law* was one such program, and it ran from 1986 to 1994. Its cast included Harry Hamlin, Corbin Bernsen, Susan Ruttan, Jimmy Smits, and Susan Dey. *L.A. Law* portrayed legal work as interesting, well-paid, and of generally high social stature. It was set in a prestigious Los Angeles law firm where everyone looked attractive and had engaging personal lives. A top-level attorney in the United States earned up to $91,690 in 1985, but median earnings were in the mid-$40,000 range, which was in line with salaries earned by other professional groups.[45] The attorneys depicted in *L.A. Law* were living exceptional professional lives compared to actual lawyers across the United States.[46]

Gender played an important role in American television in the 1980s, and perhaps no show better illustrated this reality than *Murphy Brown*. It ran from 1988 to 1998 and starred Candice Bergen as the title character. The show was set in a television newsroom and Brown worked as a renowned broadcaster. The character was in many ways an updated version of Mary Tyler Moore's Mary Richards, and *Murphy Brown* was popular because of the humor that was used to show the challenges of being a working professional woman who also became a single parent.[47]

While attorneys and physicians continued to be popular subjects for dramatic television, there were other professional occupations that were largely absent. Dramas and sitcoms about engineers, accountants, everyday managers, or scientists did not appear on network broadcast schedules. Shows that featured teachers also lost favor in Hollywood. Producers and television executives clearly concluded that the public was interested in fictional depictions of medical and legal work and responded accordingly. These trends helped reinforce what occupations should be considered socially important and those that were not.

Police and First Responders

Police and first responder work was as popular on 1980s television as it had been during the 1970s, and such shows began to evolve and feature a more diverse cast of characters. It was also supposed to show the real lives of police officers and daily workplace challenges that they faced. *Hill Street Blues* was produced by Steven Bochco as new type of grittier police drama. It had a large cast that altered slightly during the show's six-year run. The directors and producers often covered several plotlines in each episode, and the method of shooting the show was different due to the use of hand-held cameras.[48]

It was never clear in what city *Hill Street Blues* was set, and that was a deliberate decision by the show's producers as they wanted it to represent any big American city. It mostly resembled either New York City or Chicago, and it was actually filmed in Los Angeles. The cast included some characters that verged on caricature. Grizzled senior sergeants were played by Michael Conrad and Robert Prosky, Daniel J. Travanti was a stoic captain, Veronica Hamel as public defender Joyce Davenport, Bruce Weitz as a slightly unhinged detective, and Taurean Blacque as another detective. The public liked the seemingly realistic portrayal of police work shown on *Hill Street Blues* and the series won many Emmy awards and nominations. It seemed as though it had ushered in a new way of showing police work, but other more stylized police shows also appeared in the 1980s.

Women's roles in police dramas changed in the 1980s, and it was an overdue update to better reflect the evolving nature of police work. *Cagney and Lacey* was on CBS from 1982 to 1988. It starred Sharon Gless as Christine Cagney and Tyne Daley as Mary Beth Lacey as New York City police detectives. Depicting police working as partners was an established practice in Hollywood by this time, and it mirrored actual police work practice. Cagney was single and focused on her career, while Lacey was a married working mother.[49]

Cagney and Lacey was supposed to present a realistic portrayal of what it meant to be a woman working as a police detective, and it focused on both the personal and professional lives of the main characters. The characters had to juggle their work and private lives, and neither was living an extravagant lifestyle on their police salaries. Both Gless and Daley won Emmy awards for their portrayals of Cagney and Lacey, and the show enjoyed a reasonably long run on network television. It may well have had the effect of encouraging women to pursue police work as a career.

The 1980s are now commonly viewed as a decade of excess, and no program better-exemplified excess than *Miami Vice*. It ran from 1984 to 1989 and revolved around the professional lives of two Miami Police Department detectives: Sonny Crockett and Ricardo Tubbs, with Don Johnson playing Crockett and Philip Michael Thomas as Tubbs. The show was highly stylized, with the two detectives driving around in a Ferrari. This was ostensibly to assist with undercover work, but Crockett and Tubbs were never seen routinely riding around in everyday unmarked police cars. They were dressed in expensive clothing, always in the company of beautiful women, and in conflict with criminals that often involved a lot of shooting without necessarily an equal amount of mortality. There was never any discussion in *Miami Vice* of how much money police detectives made, and the overall impression conveyed through the film was that police work was mostly glamorous, often dangerous, and never dull.[50]

There were representations of law enforcement work that were also outside of the usual bounds of police and other such agencies. The private investigator became a popular figure in American television since the medium's inception. A radio and later TV show called *Martin Kane, Private Eye* ran on Mutual and NBC from 1949 to 1954. The attraction of the private investigator figure seems to be that it is usually a man who may have formally been a police officer of some rank who now, often for unexplained reasons, almost operates as a legal vigilante. Working as a private investigator is entirely legal in the United States, although it does often require passing a licensing test and having some prior related experience.[51]

There were two series that exemplified the private eye genre in the 1970s and 1980s—it is appropriate to describe them together at this point in the narrative—and they presented vastly different depictions of the nature of private investigation work. *The Rockford Files* was on NBC from 1974 to 1980. It starred James Garner as Los Angeles PI Jim Rockford. Rockford routinely finds work in the series, but he lives a decidedly modest lifestyle. He owns a trailer that he has parked near the ocean in Malibu and drives a brown Chevrolet Camaro. His father, a retired truck driver named Rocky played by Noah Beery Jr., is his closest confidant. Rockford has a somewhat motley collection of characters around him who sometimes hinder more than help him, such as petty conman Angel Martin played by Stuart Margolin. The recurring cast was mostly comprised of people who worked to just get by economically, while usually displaying some wry humor along the way.[52]

Nostalgia also appeared in the private investigator genre when CBS premiered *Mickey Spillane's Mike Hammer* in 1984.[53] Spillane was a thriller writer and the Hammer character first appeared in 1947 in the novel *I, The Jury*.[54] The 1984 version of Hammer was played by Stacey Keach, and the character verged on private eye caricature. He always wore a suit and fedora hat and liked big band music. The producers intended Hammer to be a character that reminded viewers of the 1940s; a man's man who fought crime with both fists and was always liked by attractive women.

Thomas Magnum was in many ways the polar opposite to Jim Rockford, and perhaps closer to Mike Hammer. Magnum was the lead character in *Magnum PI*, which was on CBS from 1980 to 1988. It starred Tom Selleck as Magnum, John Hillerman as Jonathan Higgins, Roger E. Mosley as T.C., and Larry Manetti as Rick Wright. Magnum lived on the Hawai'i estate of mysterious author Robin Masters, drove around Oahu in a red Ferrari, and encountered far more interesting adversaries than Jim Rockford. Magnum was a Vietnam War veteran and former US Navy officer, so there was also some mystery in his past. *Magnum PI* made working as a private investigator seem glamorous and exciting, even if it was unclear how exactly he paid his bills. 1970s TV showed that women could also be private investigators. *Charlie's Angels* ran from 1976 to 1981 and starred Farah Fawcett as Jill Munroe, Kate Jackson as Sabrina Duncan, and Jaclyn Smith as Kelly Garrett. They were employed by a Los Angeles detective agency owned by Charles Townsend, a character whose face was never seen in the show but whose voice was provided by John Forsythe. The three women went on weekly adventures fighting crime. The show was a great commercial success during its run on ABC.[55]

An unbelievable depiction of private investigator work was seen in *Knight Rider*, which featured David Hasselhoff as Michael Knight. It ran on NBC from 1982 to 1986 and involved Knight fighting crime from a highly advanced and talking Pontiac Trans Am. Rockford's Camaro was a companion model to the Trans Am but was clearly much less advanced compared to Knight's car. In the case of *Knight Rider*, being a PI was almost a fantasy experience. The show was influenced by spy films such as the James Bond series.[56]

Working as a private investigator was not realistically depicted in *Magnum PI* or *Night Rider*, but 1980s viewers wanted escapism in their television programming as much as they wanted realism. They got a lot of the former in *Baywatch*. This series included a large cast and was about lifeguards working on the beach in Malibu, and it initially premiered on NBC in 1989. David Hasselhoff is also in *Baywatch* as Mitch Buchannon along with Pamela Anderson as C.J. Parker, Parker Stevenson as Craig Pomeroy, Yasmine Bleeth as Caroline Holden, and several other rotating cast members. It did not initially attract a strong viewership but eventually became somewhat of a cultural sensation as it was alternately loved and mocked. Anyone watching *Baywatch* received a decidedly skewed view of working as a lifeguard. Seemingly mundane details like income and living conditions were glossed over in favor of portraying lifeguards as emergency response professionals equal to uniformed personnel. The fact that the cast was universally in good physical condition and clad in form-fitting bathing suits helped fuel the show's appeal.[57]

Humor and Work

1980s television depicted workers from different occupational groups interacting in a way that had not always happened in prior decades. Prime-time series further depicted people from more ethnically they and racially diverse backgrounds in jobs that had not previously been seen doing on TV. In casting a diverse group of workers, no show did a better job of it than *Cheers*. It was set in a Boston bar of the same name, and it showed people both working and sharing their working time off the job. It was highly humorous and had a loyal viewership during its run from 1982 to 1993.[58]

The main characters in the first years of *Cheers* were bar owner Sam Malone played by Ted Danson and wait staff Diane Chambers and Carla Torelli played by Shelley Long and Rhea Perlman. The show's cast featured key supporting characters such as Kelsey Grammer's Fraser Crane, John Ratzenberger's Cliff Claven, and George Wendt as Norm Peterson. The show was not racially diverse but was in terms of occupations mentioned in it. Malone is a former relief pitcher for the Boston Red Sox, Chambers is a graduate student at Boston University, Crane a psychiatrist, Peterson an accountant, Torelli a career waitress, and Claven a US Postal Service employee. There were no barriers between any of the characters due to social class; indeed differences in occupation helped drive the overall comic narrative.

Depictions of racialized workers altered in the 1980s when compared with the preceding decade. Shows like *Sanford and Son* that used comedy to describe low-wage work were out and new programs that went far beyond *The Jeffersons* and its themes of upward Black socio-economic mobility were in. *The Cosby Show* was a successor to *The Jeffersons* even if producer and star Bill Cosby himself did not readily acknowledge this detail. *The Cosby Show* premiered in 1984 and was on NBC for eight years. It was about Dr. Cliff Huxtable, an obstetrician played by Cosby, his attorney wife Claire Huxtable played by Phylicia Rashad, and their children.[59]

The show was set in Brooklyn and it showed a successful Black family led by professionals. *The Cosby Show* included serious topics such as teen pregnancy in its plots, but it was first and foremost a comedy based on Bill Cosby's own standup routines. The show may have mistakenly led white audiences to conclude that poverty and other problems were no longer experienced by the Black community, but it was also enormously popular. It certainly changed the perceptions that white people had of the work done by Black Americans. The clearly negative aspect of *The Cosby Show* is related to revelations after it ended about Bill Cosby's sexual impropriety and the legal consequences that he later faced because of it.

The white working class may have fallen into the television background for much of the 1980s or was part of ensemble casts from different occupational backgrounds, but it came back to the forefront toward the end of the decade with *Roseanne*. This comedy was about working blue-collar mother Roseanne Conner, created by Roseanne Barr, and her family.

The other main cast members were John Goodman as husband Dan Conner and their children Becky played by Lecy Goranson, Darlene played by Sara Gilbert, and D.J. played by Michael Fishman. The Conners lived outside of Chicago and faced a raft of financial challenges. Roseanne is working at a plastics factory at the start of the series and Dan is a construction contractor. The show's producers, including Roseanne Barr herself, devoted a lot of attention to thinking about the working lives of the main and supporting characters along with their personal lives.[60]

The end of the 1980s brought another comedy that was similar to *Roseanne*. *Married ... With Children* premiered in 1987 and had a ten-year run on Fox. It centered on shoe salesman Al Bundy played by Ed O'Neill, his wife Peggy played by Katey Sagal, and children Kelly and Bud played by Christina Applegate and David Faustino. It was set in the Chicago suburbs. *Married ... With Children* brought a comedic critique of working-class America toward the end of the twentieth century much as *Roseanne* did. The Bundy family struggled with money, although the women in the family were portrayed in a less positive manner than seen in *Roseanne*. The women in *Roseanne* were stronger figures, especially Roseanne herself, while Sagal's and Applegate's characters were shown as materialistic and somewhat shallow.[61]

The 1980s came to end with the beginning of the longest-running comedy series ever made in the United States: *The Simpsons*. It is an adult-oriented cartoon that has run continually since 1989. The show features Homer, Marg, Bart, Lisa, and Maggie Simpson. It was conceived of by Matt Groening, and he based the characters on his own family. Work and labor are routinely included in the show. Homer works as a safety inspector at a nuclear plant, while Marg has occasionally been employed. Many of Homer's mishaps involve events at work, and he is often at odds with his boss C. Montgomery Burns. The Simpsons may well be the most famous working-class family in the history of American television.[62]

Generational Change

The generational changes that began in the 1960s with the baby boomers leaving high school continued to evolve, and that generation had become middle-aged parents by the 1980s. The angst facing the boomers and their interaction with their own children provided useful fodder for both comedic and dramatic television scripts. *Family Ties* premiered on NBC in 1982 and ran until 1989. It starred Michael Gross and Meredith Baxter as Steven and Elyse Keaton, Michael J. Fox and Brian Bonsall as their sons Alex and Andrew, and Justin Bateman and Tina Yothers as daughters Mallory and Jennifer. *Family Ties* included references to the working lives of Steven and Elyse, with Steven working as a manager at a local public broadcasting station and Elyse an architect.[63]

The Keatons were almost a reverse version of the 1970s Bunkers. Both parents worked, while women in 1970s TV programs were often working full-time out of necessity rather than personal preference. Differences in political outlook were the most marked difference in the fictional Keaton household. Whereas conservative-minded Archie Bunker argued with his liberal daughter and son-in-law, the liberal baby boom Keaton parents had to cope with their enthusiastically Generation X Republican son Alex. Fox's portrayal of Alex Keaton became somewhat of a 1980s cultural icon, and viewers were attracted by the interplay between the formerly hippie parents and their conservative son. Alex Keaton was not out to pursue social justice and instead was fixated on making as much money as possible.

The baby boomers were a natural TV constituency in the 1980s. That cohort was born between 1946 and 1964, and they were firmly in their thirties in the 1980s and they liked seeing themselves on screen. No 1980s series was more clearly targeted at boomers than *Thirtysomething*. It was first broadcast on ABC in 1987 and ran until 1991. The main characters included Ken Olin as Michael Steadman, Mel Harris as Hope Murdoch Steadman, Timothy Busfield as Elliot Weston, and Patricia Wettig as Nancy Krieger Weston. There were several other supporting characters. Mel and Hope wanted to be writers, but she stayed home doing domestic work when they had children and he worked in advertising. Elliot works in graphic design, and Nancy stays home to look after their kids then subsequently works as an illustrator of children's books.[64]

Working life and pressures of performing both paid and unpaid work, the alienation that comes from being engaged in a career that is not your first choice, and the hurdle of returning to work after a lengthy absence are all shown in *Thirtysomething*. There were nonetheless some issues with how it portrayed working life and the baby boomers who were in their prime working years. The cast was overwhelmingly white, like so many other shows made during the 1980s, and it was about educated middle-class people. This aspect of it made *Thirtysomething* more escapist than realistic, but the show's creators clearly intended it for viewers who looked like the characters shown in it.

Television and Work in the Age of Stagflation and Reagan

Changes in working life were found in many TV shows produced in the 1970s and 1980s, although work was sometimes more clearly evident in some programs than in others. The shift away from making shows that put the working class as the center of fictional narratives gave way to making the middle class and its managerial and professional members more prominent. Humor was effectively used to buttress plotlines about low-paid and highly gendered work, upward social mobility, and social class. The same kinds of themes had been found in films, and they were also the inspiration for music.

Notes

1 *All in the Family*, created by Norman Lear, 1971–1979, CBS Television.
2 Smithsonian, "Archie Bunker's Chair from All in the Family," National Museum of American History, accessed 1 November 2023, https://www.si.edu/object/archie-bunkers-chair-all-family%3Anmah_670097.
3 *Maude*, created by Norman Lear and Bud Yorkin, 1972–1978, CBS Television.
4 *The Jeffersons*, created by Don Nichol, Eric Monte, Norman Lear, Michael Ross, and Bernie West, 1975–1985, CBS Television.
5 Democracy Now!, "TV Legend Norman Lear on the Black Panthers, Nixon's Enemies List & What Gives Him Hope," 25 October 2016, https://www.democracynow.org/2016/10/25/norman_lear_on_nixons_enemies_list.
6 *Good Times*, created by Eric Monte and Mike Evans, 1974–1979, CBS Television.
7 *Sanford and Son*, created by Norman Lear and Bud Yorkin, 1972–1977, CBS Television.
8 *Steptoe and Son*, created by Ray Galton and Alan Simpson, 1962–1965, BBC 1.
9 *Sanford and Son*, created by Norman Lear and Bud Yorkin, 1972–1977, CBS Television. On the cultural significance of programs like *Sanford and Son* see Adrien Sebro, *Scratchin' and Survivin': Hustle Economics and the Black Sitcoms of Tandem Productions* (New Brunswick, NJ: Rutgers University Press, 2023).
10 *Chico and the Man*, created by James Komack, NBC, 1974–1978.
11 Malcolm X with Alex Haley, *The Autobiography of Malcolm X* (New York: Grove Press, 1965).
12 Alex Haley, *Roots: The Saga of an American Family* (New York: Doubleday, 1976).
13 *Roots*, directed by Marvin J. Chomsky, John Erman, David Greene, and Gilbert Moses, 1977, ABC Television; *Roots: The Next Generations* directed by John Erman, Charles S. Dubin, and Georg Stanford Brown, 1979, ABC Television.
14 *Gone with the Wind*, directed by Victor Fleming (1939; Los Angeles, CA: Selznick International Pictures).
15 *Adam-12*, created by Robert A. Cinader and Jack Webb, 1968-1975, NBC.
16 *Hawaii Five-O*, created by Leonard Freeman, 1968–1980, CBS.
17 *Emergency*, created by Robert A. Cinader, Harold Jack Bloom, and Jack Webb, 1972–1977, NBC.
18 *Starsky and Hutch*, created by William Blinn, 1975–1979, ABC.
19 *Barney Miller*, created by Danny Arnold and Theodore J. Flicker, 1975–1982, ABC.
20 *The Dukes of Hazzard*, created by Gy Waldron, 1975–1985, CBS.
21 *B.J. and the Bear*, created by Glen A. Larson and Christopher Crowe, 1972–1981, NBC.
22 *The Dick Van Dyke Show*, created by Carl Reiner, 1961–1966, CBS.
23 *The Mary Tyler Moore Show*, created by James L. Brooks and Allan Burns, 1970–1977, CBS.

24 *The Mary Tyler Moore Show*, Season Two, Episode 8, "Thoroughly Unmilitant Mary," directed by Jay Sandrich, aired 6 November 1971, CBS.

25 *Rhoda*, created by James L. Brooks and Allan Burns, 1974–1978, CBS.

26 *Phyllis*, created by James L Brooks, Stan Daniels, and Ed Weinberger, 1975–1977, CBS.

27 *Lou Grant*, season 4 episode 13, "Strike," directed by Gene Reynolds, aired 16 February 1981, CBS.

28 *One Day at a Time*, created by Whitney Blake and Allan Manings, 1975–1984, CBS.

29 *Alice*, created by Robert Getchell, 1976–1985, CBS.

30 *Happy Days*, created by Garry Marshall, 1974–1984, ABC.

31 *Laverne and Shirley*, created by Garry Marshall, 1976–1983, ABC.

32 *The Odd Couple*, developed by Garry Marshall and Jerry Belson, 1970–1975, ABC.

33 *The Waltons*, created by Earl Hamner Jr., 1972–1981, CBS.

34 *The Homecoming: A Christmas Story*, directed by Fielder Cook (1971; Los Angeles, CA: CBS).

35 Museum of Modern Art, "Dorothea Lange: American, 1895-1965," accessed 1 November 2023, https://www.moma.org/artists/3373.

36 *Little House on the Prairie*, developed by Blanche Hanalis, 1974–1983, NBC.

37 *Welcome Back Kotter*, created by Gabe Kaplan and Alan Sacks, 1975–1979, ABC.

38 *The White Shadow*, created by Bruce Paltrow, 1978–1981, CBS.

39 *WKRP in Cincinnati*, created by Hugh Wilson, 1978–1982, CBS.

40 *These Are My Children*, created by Irna Phillips, 1949, CBS.

41 *All My Children*, created by Agnes Nixon, 1970–2011, ABC; *As the World Turns*, created by Irna Phillips, 1956–2010, CBS; *Another World*, created by Irna Phillips and William J. Ball, 1964–1999, NBC.

42 *Coronation Street*, created by Tony Warren, 1960-present, ITV.

43 Francesca Giuliani-Hoffman, "Analysis: Why actors make for better presidents," CNN, 30 August 2017, https://www.cnn.com/2017/08/30/politics/president-reagan-trump-acting-cnn-film/index.html.

44 *St. Elsewhere*, created by Joshua Brand and John Falsey, 1982-1988, NBC.

45 Craig Prieser, "Occupational salary levels for white-collar workers, 1985," accessed 10 October 2023, Bureau of Labor Statistics, https://www.bls.gov/opub/mlr/1985/10/rpt1full.pdf.

46 *L.A. Law*, created by Stephen Bochco and Terry Louise Fisher, 1986–1994, NBC.

47 *Murphy Brown*, created by Diane English, 1988–1998, CBS.

48 *Hill Street Blues*, created by Stephen Bochco and Michael Kozoll, 1981–1987, NBC.

49 *Cagney and Lacey*, created by Barbara Avedon and Barbara Corday, 1982–1988, CBS.

50 *Miami Vice*, created by Anthony Yerkovich, 1984–1989, NBC.

51 *Martin Kane, Private Eye*, written and directed by Ted Hediger, 1949–1954, Mutual and NBC.

52 *The Rockford Files*, created by Roy Huggins and Stephen J. Cannell, 1974–1980, NBC.

53 *Mickey Spillane's Mike Hammer*, produced by Jay Bernstein, 1984-1987, CBS.

54 Mickey Spillane, *I, The Jury* (New York: E.P. Dutton, 1947).

55 *Charlie's Angels*, created by Ivan Goff and Ben Roberts, 1976–1981, CBS.

56 *Knight Rider*, created by Glen A. Larson, 1982–1986. NBC.

57 *Baywatch*, created by Michael Berk, Douglas Schwartz, and Gregory J. Bonann, NBC.
58 *Cheers*, created by Glen and Les Charles and James Burrows, 1982–1993, NBC.
59 *The Cosby Show*, created by Bill Cosby, Ed Weinberger, Michael J. Leeson, 1984–1992, NBC.
60 *Roseanne*, created by Matt Williams, 1988-1997, ABC.
61 *Married ... With Children*, created by Michael G. Moye and Ron Leavitt, 1987–1997, Fox.
62 *The Simpsons*, created by Matt Groening, 1989-present, Fox.
63 *Family Ties*, created by Gary David Goldberg, 1982–1989, NBC.
64 *Thirtysomething*, created by Edward Zwick and Marshall Herskovitz, 1987–1991, NBC.

3 Music

People have long turned to music to express their feelings about work and labor. It can be quicker to sit and write a song than to create a television series or feature film, and many artists integrated commentaries on working life into a remarkable range of music genres during the 1970s and 1980s. Describing how artists talked about work and labor is best accomplished by looking at the music that was written and released across genres, as some music endured throughout the 1970s and 1980s, while others were enormously popular for a few years before declining, with other new forms rising in popularity.

This chapter is different than the two that preceded it as it incorporates discussion of music made by people outside of the United States. This is because music from the United Kingdom and other countries was popular with American audiences in a way that overseas television and film were not similarly embraced. A band like The Police had two English members and one American. Musicians acknowledged influences across borders in a way that film and television creators did not readily admit when their work was inspired by work made in another country.

Many stories about working life were told through music during the 1970s and 1980s, and the music industry altered over those years because of new genres but also because of changes in technology. This was a significant contrast with the film and television industries. The rise of videocassette recorders (VCRs) and VHS (Video Home System) and Beta format videotapes influenced how people watched films and TV shows, but that technology actually had a positive impact. Film studios found that they could sell copies of movies after they had theatrical runs, and they could also sell copies of their back catalogs. TV producers also found that they could sell series that were no longer broadcast. There were concerns that making it possible for people to tape and watch a television episode potentially harmed reruns, but videotaping was not as disruptive as feared. It had the effect of creating the video rental store as a new retail segment.[1]

DOI: 10.4324/9781003384564-4

The music business entered the 1970s distributing music on vinyl 45 rpm singles and 33 1/3 rpm albums, cassette tapes, and 8-track cartridges. 8-tracks were gone by the end of the 1980s and the compact disc (CD) was quickly becoming the dominant format. The way that people consumed music also changed with the creation of better portable music technology. Sony developed the Walkman, a wearable cassette tape player with lightweight headphones, in 1979 and they were ubiquitous by the end of the 1980s. Car stereos became more sophisticated during the 1970s and 1980s. These changes in technology, combined with the profusion of music genres available by the end of the 1980s, meant that people could even listen to music about work while at work. Music could be part of a person's everyday life with greater ease than sitting in front of a television or in a movie theater.

A key challenge with music genres and formats in the 1970s and 1980s was that they served to bifurcate the wider music-listening audience. People could choose whatever genre they preferred and even listen by themselves through headphones. A person could also sit alone in a movie theater or in front of a television, but the effect was not as significant as it could be with music. Music became divided by race and class with country music being overwhelmingly associated with white artists and fans, rap with Black artists and initially Black fans, punk with white artists and fans, with rock and roll being a primarily white form rooted in Black music. Messages about work and labor thus came from different genres, although the various forms of music drew on each other more than some artists may have wanted to admit.

The 1970s

Country Music

Country music often readily comes to mind when thinking about work and labor in music, and the 1970s were a period when country was more of a niche genre than it would be by the late 1980s. It emerged in the American South and the term "country music" came into popular usage in the 1940s. Country's roots were a combination of European and African influences that were shaped by the immigrant and American rural and frontier experiences. Although it has included artists who came from across the United States, country has become mainly associated with the South, Mid-West, and Western states and it is from those regions that the more well-known country music artists originated.

Country appeared to become more conservative in the 1970s due to the themes in its songs and the public personas of its leading performers. Charlie Pride was the only well-known Black country artist, and everyone else seemed to be a white person with working-class roots. Merle Haggard was a performer who exemplified those traits. Haggard was from a small town near Bakersfield, California. One of the major misconceptions of the Small counterculture era was that California was a bastion of Hippie liberalism, when in fact the inland regions of the state were more likely to be strongly conservative. Haggard wrote and released "Okie from Muskogee" late in 1969 and it was a hit song into 1970. It was viewed as a negative critique of Small counterculture beliefs and celebrated conservative, small-town life. This was the kind of place where increasingly conservatively minded American blue-collar workers lived while they looked askance at how many young people opposed established authority during the Vietnam years.[2]

Haggard was a young performer in 1970, and there were others who were more established in the country music business that integrated work and labor themes into their songs. Johnny Cash wrote and performed many songs about working-class life in the United States including what it was like being incarcerated in "Folsom Prison Blues".[3] Cash's 1973 recorded "Oney", which was about a blue-collar worker who plans to throw a punch at his boss after tolerating abusive behavior for years.[4] Cash and Haggard wrote songs that were tributes to the average working person, but other artists wrote songs that had more overt protest mentioned in them.

The music business has been replete with one-hit wonders—acts that had one popular song—since it began. Some songs briefly captured attention and were regarded as novelty recordings, but they also revealed something about society and culture at the time they were released. "Convoy" was by C.W. McCall and released in 1975. It was essentially a spoken word recording with a chorus of singers. McCall's real name was William Dale Fries, Jr. and he had an eclectic career that included being elected mayor of a town in Colorado.[5]

"Convoy" is linked to the brief mid-1970s popularity of truck driver culture and Citizen's Band (CB) radios that were used by long-haul truckers. The song's lyrics were simplistic and talked about assembling a convoy of trucks to travel across the United States on an unspecified mission. It associated a particular occupation—truck driving—with anti-establishment sentiment. It was decidedly anti-government as the lyrics described challenging the police and national guard. The song had an up-tempo beat but it did not mask the sinister undertones of the lyrics. "Convoy" was a song to which people could easily listen because the lyrics and chorus were clearly stated and sung, and it was essentially a mid-1970s protest song that fed into post-Vietnam disenchantment felt by a more conservative segment of society.

Anti-establishment messages were also central to Johnny Paycheck's 1977 song "Take This Job and Shove It". This song had a reasonably fast tempo and was viewed as somewhat humorous due to its chorus. A closer reading of the lyrics reveals that it was in fact about a man who had worked in a factory for 40 years whose wife had left him, and who is now ready to "blow his top" at management. Many blue-collar men surely heard some of their own working experience in Paycheck's lyrics. This was not the last time that the meaning of a song about working life in the 1970s and 1980s was misconstrued by listeners.[6]

Jerry Reed wrote and performed "Eastbound and Down" in 1977, and it was about a trucker running bootleg beer.[7] Mel Tillis released "Sawmill" in 1973 as a commentary on working in a sawmill.[8] Comparing such songs shows the contrast of doing work that is legal but feeling worn down by it with celebrating work that is based on illegal work. Songs were also occasionally written about working as a performer. Glenn Campbell's 1975 "Rhinestone Cowboy" became his best-known song, and it was about his life as a performer and the feelings of loneliness and even alienation that could come with the job.[9]

Some memorable work and labor country songs of the 1970s were written and performed by women. The start of the 1970s coincided with the release of Loretta Lynn's landmark song "Coal Miner's Daughter".[10] Lynn was born poor in the early years of the Depression in Kentucky, and her father had been a coal miner. The song was a commentary on living and working in rural Kentucky and the challenges that Lynn's family faced. It was the inspiration for a 1980 biographical film also titled *Coal Miner's Daughter* that starred Sissy Spacek as Lynn.[11] That film garnered positive reviews, and it was notably directed by English director Michael Apted. Apted made several Hollywood films but was perhaps best known for the documentary *Up* series of films that chronicled the lives of a group of British youth as they grew into adulthood. Country music written by men and women influenced other genres in the 1970s.

Rock and Roll

The term "rock and roll" was first used in the context of music by disc jockey Alan Freed in the 1950s. Rock's complex roots led it to diverge into sub-genres in the 1970s. Bands that were heavily influenced by country music integrated it into rock songs. They later influenced the new country sound that began to appear by the late 1980s. No band better exemplified this trend than the Eagles. This band had Don Henley, Glenn Frey, Joe Walsh, Randy Misener, and Don Felder in its original lineup. The Eagles actually began as the band for Linda Ronstadt, and they formally adopted their name in 1971.[12]

The Eagles recorded key 1970s albums including *Hotel California* and *The Eagles Greatest Hits*.[13] One of the most clearly work-related songs they recorded was "Take It Easy" from their 1972 debut eponymous album.[14] The song was co-written by Glenn Frey and Jackson Browne and was another 1970s song that included truck-driving themes. It could have easily been a country song—it was later covered by country performer Travis Tritt—and became associated with any sort of work that involved driving.

Jackson Browne Work also penned "The Load-Out" as a commentary on the experience of being on the road touring.[15] His lyrics included the perspectives of the performer and the road crew that kept a tour moving along. Work themes were central to certain songs by Styx, most notably "Blue Collar Man (Long Nights)".[16] That 1978 song was about a blue-collar worker who stood in an unemployment benefits line while reflecting on his life struggles. Bob Seger sang "Feel Like a Number" in 1978.[17] Seger described a man working late and feeling pain because of it, being anonymous to his boss, and otherwise just being a number rather than a person with an identity.

An R&B artist—Tina Turner—covered a Credence Clearwater Revival (CCR) song called "Proud Mary" in 1970. She and her then husband Ike Turner included it on their album *Workin' Together*. "Proud Mary" was about moving on from difficult times and hard work, with lyrics about leaving "A good job in the city" after "Workin' for the man every night and day". It became a signature song for Tina Turner more than it was for CCR.[18]

Rock and Roll songs are often about love gained and lost, but it includes a sub-genre that has few love songs: progressive rock. Prog rock, as it is often called, includes acts from the United Kingdom and the United States. It was a form of music that was made possible by changes in recording technology. The number of tracks that could be recorded and combined into a single song expanded by the 1970s. In contrast to the 1960s, which saw an evolution from 4-track to 8-track recording technology, recording in 24–32-track formats became possible. This evolution meant that music with more complex production values could be recorded.

The United States was home to prog rock bands, but the more prominent acts came from the United Kingdom. Kansas is an example of an American band that is associated with prog rock. The band was founded in 1973 in Kansas and enjoyed chart success with songs like "Carry On Wayward Son" and "Dust in the Wind".[19] Like most prog rock bands, the members of Kansas came from more middle-class backgrounds, and while Kansas songs were about social alienation, they did not talk about the working-class experience. Kansas did write and perform songs about personal relationships, but the band became mainly known for hits like "Carry On Wayward Son" and "Dust in the Wind".[20]

Pink Floyd is perhaps the most famed of the prog rock bands, and its prominence is directly related to the number of albums it sold. Pink Floyd continues to be influential into the twenty-first century. It was comprised of four men from mostly middle-class English backgrounds, and their music focused on working life and the prospects and perils that a person could encounter depending on a chosen career path. "Money" from the 1973 album *Dark Side of the Moon* is a meditation on the pursuit of material wealth.[21] "Welcome to the Machine" and "Have a Cigar" are included in 1975's *Wish You Were Here* and both have lyrics that describe dealing with bureaucracy and the potential consequences of material success.[22] Both songs were informed by the band's experience with the music industry. Prog rock is often thought to have a more sophisticated listening audience, and it has bourgeois roots. An audience can also be sophisticated if it just wants to have a good time.

A lot of the music created in the 1970s was serious, like prog rock, but there were works that were intended to be purely entertaining. The soundtrack to *Grease* was one of those works.[23] The film itself, described in the first chapter, was a classic boy meets girl love story. The content of the soundtrack was a contrast with the actual film. Whereas work themes are evident in the film, they were only clearly described in one song called "Beauty School Dropout" performed by Frankie Avalon.[24] The song would be regarded as sexist if it was released in the twenty-first century and is about a young woman who does not finish beauty school for undefined reasons. Being a beautician was a female working-class occupation in the 1970s and was considered an option for young women whom education officials felt had no other useful skills.

Disco

Disco was a creation of the 1970s, and it was about material excess and having a good time. Like prog rock, disco was made possible by advances in recording technology.[25] The exact start of disco and the release of the first disco song cannot be definitively identified, but the term "disco" was in use by 1974, and it was derived from discotheque.[26] Disco incorporated funk, rhythm and blues, rock, and other influences. There were artists who wrote songs about work, but disco was also an escape from it. The theme song to *Car Wash* by Rose Royce was heavily influenced by funk and R&B and was regarded as a disco song.[27] Pat Lundy recorded "Work Song" in 1977 as an soul/disco song about being worn down by daily toil.[28]

Disco also gave Americans a view into gay urban culture in the 1970s. Discos were popular with gay men. The Village People were the most visible manifestations of gay culture in disco. They were an interracial group of six men dressed in costumes—including a cowboy, construction worker, and pilot—who were basically a one-hit wonder with the song "YMCA". That song was briefly very popular and even became a sing-along favorite at sports stadiums and arenas. Dressing the band members as different occupations added to their audience appeal.[29]

The escapism of disco is most clearly seen in the songs from *Saturday Night Fever*. The soundtrack album, with the Bee Gees as the most prominent artists on it, was more popular than the film itself. It was added to the National Recording Registry in the US Library of Congress, such is its enduring cultural impact. The songs were about relationships, urban life, and just about anything other than being on the job. As noted in the first chapter, the film was all about trying to break free of a limited working-class existence to achieve greater material success and freedom.[30]

The soundtrack to *Flashdance* was essentially the last time that disco was popular and, like the *Saturday Night Fever* soundtrack, it was about escapism from physical labor and a working-class life. Disco briefly continued into the 1980s and would eventually influence music again in the twenty-first century, and its decline was unexpected in the music industry and perhaps among music listeners. What rose in popularity was completely unexpected, except by the people who were part of it.[31]

Punk

Punk rock seemed to come out of nowhere when it began getting radio play in the mid-1970s, and like most music genres, it is hard to pinpoint its actual inception. The first use of the term "punk" is attributed to Ed Sanders, who in 1970 described his album as punk rock in the *Chicago Tribune*.[32] It was shaped by artists on both sides of the Atlantic Ocean, with both American and British influences. The first punk band may well have been The Stooges, who were formed in Michigan and first played in Detroit in 1967.[33] There is some irony in this fact considering that Detroit was the home of Motown Records, and Motown artists most certainly did not sound like punk acts.

Of the 1970s punk acts, The Ramones became the American act most synonymous with the genre. They formed in New York City in 1974 and are often considered one of the first official punk acts because of their sound. The punk sound was about ultimately about defying authority and being a social outsider. The Ramones came from middle and working-class backgrounds and wrote short, fast-paced songs about the youth culture they knew. Punk was a look as much as a sound, and the Ramones looked and sounded different from new bands in the early and mid-1970s. Their counterparts in the United Kingdom were much the same in that regard.[34]

The Sex Pistols were formed in 1975 and The Clash in 1976. Both bands defined with punk era with the Ramones, although there were other acts that also made contributions. The Clash were better musicians than the other two bands. Indeed, the Sex Pistols were essentially the creation of English cultural figure Malcolm McLaren and they were poor musicians when they started. The music the Sex Pistols and The Clash wrote and performed was highly political, and often commented on working and living conditions in the United Kingdom. The United Kingdom had largely and out of necessity let go of its empire by the 1970s, joined the European Community, and dealt with economic stagnation. Unemployment was especially high among British youth, the country was deindustrializing, and it all led to social alienation that found an outlet through punk music.[35]

Punk essentially lasted for a decade. It continued to have influence after the end of the 1970s and would impact later bands like Green Day. If disco was about escapism and material success, punk stood in opposition to material success and was a relentless commentary on the realities of daily existence. In that regard, it was linked to another genre that had roots in both the United States and the United Kingdom: heavy metal.

Heavy Metal

Heavy metal's origins are directly rooted in England although metal originated in rock, which itself is rooted in the blues. Metal thus has direct British roots and indirect American origins. Led Zeppelin is often regarded as the first metal band, but it is also regarded as a rock group. Black Sabbath is a better band to describe as the first metal act. The term "heavy metal" is a nineteenth-century reference to cannon or gunpowder and was mentioned in the lyrics of Steppenwolf's 1968 song "Born to Be Wild". The term gradually entered music industry and media usage.[36]

Black Sabbath was a working-class band from industrial Birmingham and Tony Iommi, Ozzie Osbourne, Geezer Butler, and Bill Ward were its members. The band was founded in 1968. Guitarist Iommi actually left a sheet metal apprenticeship before becoming a full-time musician and had lost the tips of two fingers on his right hand on his last day in the factory. The prospect of spending life doing industrial work was sufficient impetus for the members of Black Sabbath to try being professional musicians. Iommi later commented in an interview that the sounds the band members heard working in factories influenced their music, especially Bill Ward's drum sound.[37]

Metal songs did not frequently address workplace themes, and they instead were narratives on how they and their peers from industrial communities thought about their lives. The songs are frequently dark, fatalistic, defiant, and often with an overt or covert current of violence in them. Such themes were fully evident in Black Sabbath songs like "Paranoid", "War Pigs", and "Iron Man". Bands chose names for themselves that sounded sinister and ran against what would initially seem marketable. The metal genre would later be accused of misogyny as it expanded into sub-genres. It particularly altered during the 1980s, as new sub-genres rose and others declined.[38]

The 1980s

Country Music

Country music changed as the 1980s progressed. The decade opened with more traditional acts that people would see and hear if they tuned in to the *Grand Ole Opry* television show and it concluded with the emergence of what became new country. The music began to integrate more rock influences, and some acts were considered crossovers between the two genres. Work and labor themes continued to be found in country as the 1980s passed.[39]

Dolly Parton's "9 to 5" from the film of the same name is an example of a crossover song that performed well on more than one music chart.[40] The song was like the film in that it was a narrative about juggling time commitments, getting on the job, and having to deal with a difficult boss. George Strait began his career in the 1980s with songs such as "All My Exes Live in Texas".[41] His 1982 recording of "Amarillo by Morning" is about a trucker who has seemingly lost everything but still had his freedom.[42] There was also the basic fact that rural and farming life was central to the country genre, and farming meant being self-employed. The 1980s were a time when American farms were in a period of crisis. Willie Nelson, Neil Young, and John Mellencamp—the latter two crossover artists who performed rock and country—organized the first Farm Aid concert in 1985 to raise funds to support struggling family farms across the United States.[43] This was an instance of musicians endeavoring to help other workers. Farm Aid has continued into the twenty-first century.

Rock and Roll

The music industry and the messages that it conveyed were forever altered on August 1, 1981 when Music Television (MTV) debuted. The first video it broadcast was "Video Killed the Radio Star" by English band The Buggles, and while video did not kill radio, it did provide an entirely new way of engaging with popular music. There were short films and videos that featured songs before MTV, but this was a channel that was devoted entirely to music videos and news. It also facilitated the rise of new genres and acts that may not have gained popularity without it.[44]

Without question, the 1980s marked the rise to superstardom of an American performer who consistently included work and labor themes into his work: Bruce Springsteen. Springsteen first came to the attention of the music industry with the 1973 album *Greetings from Asbury Park*.[45] He grew up in a working-class New Jersey family and that experience informed what he wanted to accomplish as a musician. Springsteen's third album, *Born to Run*, was full of songs about hope and loss and the title track and other songs on the album became enduring hits.[46] What he wrote in the 1970s led to three albums in the 1980s that defined Springsteen as America's chronicler of working life in the 1970s and 1980s.

The River was released in 1980 and was full of themes about the decline of working-class life in the north-eastern states. Springsteen wrote the title track as a tribute to his sister and brother-in-law, and it was a commentary on the working-class experience. High school sweethearts marry young out of necessity, the young man gets a unionized job in an industrial facility, and their dreams are accordingly adjusted. *The River* described issues of generational change and difference on the track "Independence Day" and existence and death on "Cadillac Ranch". It was an ambitious double album and did well on the album charts. It captured white working-class life in the United States as the Reagan era began.[47]

Nebraska came out in 1982. The Vietnam War was clearly on Springsteen's mind when the tracks for this album were composed. "Highway Patrolman" is about a man who was working as a farmer and took a job as a highway patrol officer out of economic necessity. He ends up having to deal with criminal activity perpetrated by his Vietnam War veteran brother. "Johnny 99" tells the story of a laid-off auto worker who is sentenced to 99 years in prison after committing murder while drunk, then requests to be executed rather than face a life sentence. Springsteen increasingly incorporated work and labor themes into his songs through *The River* and *Nebraska*; the next album went even further.[48]

Born in the U.S.A. was Springsteen's seventh studio album and released in 1984. It was his most commercially oriented album, and it was hugely successful with seven of the songs rising into a top ten position on the sales charts. It is also one of the most misinterpreted rock albums ever created in the United States. Listeners initially thought they were hearing an album of patriotic songs, but it was in fact another Springsteen critique of the challenges of working life in America. Most of the songs or the videos that accompanied them were about work and labor themes and did not seem overtly patriotic. Springsteen instead presented a different type of patriotism by describing what was wrong in the United States and the need to address issues like deindustrialization.[49]

The title track became the most misunderstood song on a misinterpreted album. *Born in the U.S.A.* was about a blue-collar worker who felt alienated from contemporary society. He had fought in Vietnam.

Born in the U.S.A. was incorrectly interpreted as a patriotic song, especially by the political right. That embrace included favorable commentary from Ronald Reagan.[50] It became a sports arena anthem, with fans in the stands belting out its chorus. Springsteen himself was aware that the visual and audio imagery of the album could be interpreted in different ways, telling *Rolling Stone* magazine:

> Well, we had the flag on the cover because the first song was called "Born in the U.S.A.," and the theme of the record kind of follows from the themes I've been writing about for at least the last six or seven years. But the flag is a powerful image, and when you set that stuff loose, you don't know what's gonna' be done with it.[51]

Several songs on *Born in the U.S.A.*, including the title track, originated in the writing sessions for *Nebraska* so there is a direct thematic link between the two albums. *Born in the U.S.A.* included other songs such as "I'm on Fire", "Glory Days", and "Working on the Highway" that also involved ruminations on working life. The lyrics for *I'm on Fire*, a song about a man desiring a woman who is with another man, are not about work but the music video was all about work and social class. Springsteen portrays an auto mechanic who frequently works on a classic Ford Thunderbird for a clearly wealthy and attractive woman whose face is never seen in the video. The song and video are full of sexual tension, and the class difference between the working-class mechanic and mysterious upper-class woman could not be clearer.[52]

"Glory Days" is about a blue-collar worker reflecting on his life since high school and reminiscing about his younger years; his glory days. The video shows Springsteen alternating between operating a pile-driving machine and fronting his band in a bar. The video makes the song more explicitly about working life, but because of the song's tempo and rousing chorus, the message was somewhat lost although not nearly to the same extent as with *Born in the U.S.A.* "Working on the Highway" is about a man working on a county road crew who meets a girl at a union hall dance and subsequently gets in legal trouble.[53]

Bruce Springsteen turned somewhat away from work and labor in his next 1980s album, *Tunnel of Love*, but he was still unique compared to other rock artists in the 1980s in that his three other albums from that decade successively built on themes of work, alienation, and often loss.[54] Other major artists of the era, such as Michael Jackson on *Thriller*, did not sing about work and labor themes.[55] Springsteen became the first prominent American artist of the modern rock era to write and perform about working-class life through his three 1980s albums.

Springsteen's work was linked to work by other artists and inspired new acts coming in the music business. Bon Jovi shared a common origin with Springsteen as they were also from New Jersey. The original members—Jon Bon Jovi, Ritchie Sambora, Tico Torres, David Bryan, and Alec John Such— enjoyed enormous success with the 1986 album *Slippery When Wet*. It included "Livin' On a Prayer", a song that was much like "The River" as it was about a young couple struggling to get by while the man in the relationship has been on strike. Themes of alienation and loss were clear throughout "Livin' On a Prayer".[56]

Billy Joel is an artist who began rising to prominence around the same time as Springsteen. His work includes songs that are about work and labor themes, although not necessarily as prominently as in Springsteen's. Joel had already written "Piano Man", a song quite literally about his experience working as a piano player in a bar frequented by working-class men and women, in 1973.[57] Joel released the album *The Nylon Curtain* in 1982, and it included the song "Allentown".[58] It was an up-tempo lament for the loss of the post-World War II working-class life that so many baby boomers had known. The title was taken from Allentown, Pennsylvania, an area dependent on America's steel industry. It referenced aspects of everyday life in the mill and community. The meaning of "Allentown" was quickly grasped by listeners, and it also became an anthem for working-class life in America as everyday workers experienced economic decline.

Joel quickly followed *The Nylon Curtain* with the 1983 album *Innocent Man*.[59] This album proved to be a tremendous commercial success for Joel and it included "Uptown Girl", which was a song about a working-class man romantically pursuing a wealthy woman. The class aspect of the song was thus easily understood, and it was further reinforced by the accompanying video. Joel portrayed an auto mechanic in it, just as Springsteen later would in "I'm on Fire".[60] His then wife, supermodel Christie Brinkley, played that uptown girl in the song. It is noteworthy that both Joel and Springsteen chose to portray auto mechanics, a job associated with considerable technical skill but also exposure to dirt and grime. They were depicted in a quintessentially skilled, masculine working-class job to contrast with the attractive and immaculately upper-class dressed women in their videos.

Other artists in the 1980s followed Springsteen and Joel, often with just one song. Canadian band Loverboy wrote "Working for the Weekend" in 1981, and it became their most enduring song.[61] English band Dire Straits released "Money for Nothing" in 1985. That song was based on statements that Dire Strait's lead singer and guitar player Mark Knopfler heard a worker make while he was in an appliance store.[62] Huey Lewis and the News came out with "Workin' For a Livin'" in 1982, Donna Summer released "She Works Hard for the Money" in 1983, and The Bangles recorded "Manic Monday" in 1987.[63] That latter song is particularly interesting as it is written from the perspective of a woman waking on Monday morning and facing the prospect of the coming work week, it was performed by an all-female band, yet was written by Prince. He certainly showed his perceptiveness in that song. Jackson Browne released "Lawyers in Love" in 1983, and it was a commentary on the young urban professionals (Yuppies) who increasingly occupied the American middle and upper classes.[64]

While artists like Springsteen and Joel placed work and labor at the center of key songs they wrote and performed in the 1980s, established acts that first rose to fame in the 1960s created songs that commented on the working experience. Bob Dylan's importance in rock music is equal to acts like the Beatles, and he crossed over to rock after starting as a folk singer. His 1983 album *Infidels* included "Union Sundown", a commentary on the impact of globalization on manufacturing jobs in the United States.[65]

There was a debate within the music industry in the 1980s over the issue of licensing music for use in commercials; doing so was widely regarded as selling out to corporate America. Michael Jackson appeared in commercials for Pepsi and was grievously burned filming one. Neil Young's 1988 album *This Note's For You* included "Ten Men Workin" and title track "This Note's For You". The former song was about Young and his band working each night on stage playing music, while the latter one was a satirical commentary on artists who engage in business agreements with corporations.[66]

New Wave Acts and Other Bands

The wave of music that came across the Atlantic Ocean starting in the early 1960s has been commonly called The British Invasion, and it was to an extent replicated in the early 1980s. New wave music began at that time and it turned popular music, otherwise called pop music, in new directions. The Buggles were part of the wave. New wave was welcomed by the industry and the listening public, and punk was eclipsed by new American and British bands that sometimes performed songs that included work and labor themes. New wave and pop overall were genres that were also greatly assisted by the development of new technologies, as well as by music video. For instance, the music synthesizer became ubiquitous by the 1980s. Synthesizers had been in use prior to the 1970s and prog bands like Genesis had used them to create music, but the technology was expensive and occasionally difficult to use. Synthesizer keyboards had become cheaper, smaller, and much more usable by the 1980s and new bands made extensive use of them.

New wave included themes of both escapism and realism. English band Duran Duran were prodigious users of synthesizers and benefited considerably from being in engaging music videos. They were an example of new wave escapism and their songs were not about work and labor. In contrast, The Alarm's "Devolution Workin' Man Blues" was about a working-class man with "no money in my pocket, no soles on my shoes".[67] Other major acts that grew to prominence in the 1980s like Irish band U2 became enormously popular in the United States, yet preferred to convey other social messages through their music that did not include work and labor. English band XTC wrote about the struggles of being a young worker who must provide for his partner and child in "Earn Enough for Us".[68]

There were acts that came out in the 1980s along with New Wave but were not exactly part of that genre. R.E.M. came about the same time as new wave—although they would probably prefer to be considered a rock act—and began in Athens, Georgia. They first achieved notoriety as a college bar act before achieving national fame. Their fifth studio album, *Document*, included "Finest Worksong". It is a song about getting on with tasks in life, getting organized, and moving on and less about paid labor. In a sense, "Finest Worksong" is about the important unpaid labor done daily by everyone.[69]

There were a few music genres that did not include American acts but still influenced the US music scene and artists. Reggae is an example of such a genre, and in the 1970s it was exemplified by Bob Marley. He and his band the Wailers were from Jamaica, and America's close proximity to the Caribbean islands and the presence of a Caribbean diaspora in cities like New York meant that reggae came to America. Marley sang about work and labor themes on songs like 1980s "Work" on the album *Uprising*. Reggae artists like Marley often incorporate social commentary, so while some music is simply about having a good time, it is a genre more rooted in realism than escapism.[70]

Bands occasionally liked reflecting on life touring on the road, and The Police included "Man in a Suitcase" on their 1980 album *Zenyatta Mondatta*.[71] The song is about living out of a suitcase and hotels, generally being a stranger while moving around, and the confines of being on tour. They followed with "Synchronicity II" on 1984s *Synchronicity*.[72] That song was about how urban life and industrial work can be stifling and lead to feelings of anguish. The Police were an English and American band comprised of Sting, Stewart Copeland, and Andy Summers. Copeland is American. Sting wrote most of the band's lyrics and drew on his experience growing up in industrial Newcastle, England when composing songs.

New wave plateaued by the end of the 1980s, although acts like Duran Duran soldier on well into the twenty-first century. U2 would also likely prefer to be thought of a rock rather than new wave or pop band, and they achieved greater fame than most 1980s acts. New Wave, like disco, continued to have influence beyond the end of its decade of prominence. Another new genre that rose during the 1980s had a more enduring and transformative impact.

Hip-Hop

Spoken word format has long been part of music. It evolved in the late 1970s as hip-hop (Rap) recordings began to climb music charts. Hip-hop has diffuse origins. The term "hip-hop" is thought to have been coined by Keith Cowboy, who was a member of Grandmaster Flash and the Furious Five.[73] The Sugarhill Gang's 1979 song "Rapper's Delight" is often recognized as the first commercially successful hip-hop song, and it entered the Billboard Top 40 listing in early 1980.[74] There was also a song titled "Noah" that was recorded in 1944 by the Jubalaires that may in fact be the first recorded rap song.[75] The Sugarhill Gang put hip-hop on the music map and made a major change to the global music industry. Another aspect of hip-hop manifested itself shortly after "Rapper's Delight" came out: this new surging genre was appropriated by a white act when Blondie released "Rapture" in 1980.[76] Hip-hop incorporated R&B, rock, and disco and quickly divided into sub-genres, most notably east and west coast forms that grew into a serious rivalry after the 1980s ended.

Run-DMC were one of the first major hip-hop acts, and they were formed in Queen's, New York in 1983. The group included Jason Mizell, Darryl McDaniels, and Joseph Simmons. Early hip-hop did not outwardly celebrate conspicuous wealth and instead focused on everyday life experiences. Run-DMC's eponymous 1983 album included "Hard Times", a song that talked about difficult life challenges. The songs' lyrics included the line "All day I have to work at my peak because I need that dollar every day of the weak (sic)".[77]

Black American culture and the challenges and racism that Black people faced in America were common themes in 1980s hip-hop. Run-DMC wrote about those themes, and so did Public Enemy. Public Enemy did not explicitly write about work and labor, but they did write about economic inequality. Like Run-DMC, Public Enemy were from the east coast; specifically Long Island in the New York City area. Hip-hop acts also benefited from yet another new technology: music sampling. As time progressed, the actual music heard on hip-hop included sampled content, which basically meant taking parts of existing songs and using them in new recordings. Grandmaster Flash and the Furious Five used sampling in their 1984 song "We Don't Work for Free", which is a song that talks about being underpaid and at one point defying the US Internal Revenue Service. Hip-hop continued to grow throughout the 1980s and beyond in subsequent years. It would eventually eclipse rock in listening popularity but rock still soldiered on, as did heavy metal.[78]

Heavy Metal

Heavy metal came from the United Kingdom to the United States, and American metal bands were popular by the 1980s. Metal was like other genres as it spawned its own sub-genres including speed metal and hair metal. The latter sub-genre was more American than British, and it was a reference to hairstyle size and appearance. This was a marked contrast with bands in the 1970s that had longer hair but did not hold it in place with hairspray. American metal bands of the 1980s included Slayer and Anthrax, who were thrash metal bands, Quiet Riot, Twister Sister, and Metallica. Of that group, Metallica were the most important and had the most enduring career.

The most curious aspect of 1980s metal bands was their enormous popularity with white male youth, especially in the working class, yet they did not perform songs that reflected on work and labor themes. Metal was the preferred soundtrack for a significant slice of the young, male, working population. The music in many cases had a very dark tone, and the accompanying imagery had a similar tone. For instance, Metallica's debut album *Kill Em' All* featured a cover image of a hand holding a hammer next to a pool of blood. Some metal acts, such as former Black Sabbath lead singer Ozzy Osbourne, became less metal and more hard rock and performed occasional love ballads, but much of metal music became harder during the 1980s. It continued to be highly gendered and racialized as there were few women who achieved stardom as metal acts, and a black metal band was one that was part of an even harder-edged metal sub-genre and not one that had Black band members.[79]

Metal also had the distinction of attracting public scrutiny in a way that popular music had not since rock and roll first appeared in the 1950s. In 1985, a group called the Parents' Music Resource Center (PMRC) was formed to advocate for regulation of popular music by creating a rating system similar to the one used in the film industry. Music by metal bands including Def Leppard, Black Sabbath, and Judas Priest was identified by the PMRC as harmful for young people. The PMRC was ultimately not successful, but its activities did fuel a brief if intense discussion about the perils of censorship.[80]

Two Key Decades

The 1970s and 1980s were decades when nostalgia for America's past influenced some of the music being produced, but they were also years that produced enduring music that linked to work and labor. Rock and country existed before and after the 1970s while disco essentially came and went during the 1970s. Punk experienced a similar trajectory and was popular for a comparatively brief period and punk artists often expressed opinions on socio-economic issues.

Hip-hop took the music industry by surprise, and record companies embraced it. Hip-hop artists talked about everyday life for Black Americans. White audiences did not initially know how to interpret it, but hip-hop was primarily created for Black audiences. It did not take long for white acts to start recording hip-hop, which was what happened with rock.

Changes in technology gave people more music-listening options. Cassette tapes were not durable and were cheap to make, as are most recording formats, but they were portable and could be played on a device like a Sony Walkman. The CD is similarly portable compared with a long-play album. The transformative impact of music downloading would not be felt until the 1990s, and the 1970s and 1980s were still periods when artists as workers could earn significant incomes through writing and recording music.

Music sampling was an important change from the early 1970s to the end of the 1980s as it changed the process of making music and who called themselves musicians. A hit song could be cobbled together from bits of other songs as long as royalties were paid to the writers of those original works. Music video was the most important change to occur in the 1970s and 1980s. Acts that perhaps may have enjoyed modest popularity instead had considerable fame because of their videos. Bruce Springsteen in particular used video to add work and labor to his music.

American music in the 1970s and 1980s was not created in isolation from what was created in other countries in the same way that film and television were separate from what was created abroad. Britain was the home of metal and Americans embraced it. Reggae came from Jamaica and became popular in the United States and other countries. Punk had roots in both sides of the Atlantic, while country remained largely an American genre. Canada has produced country acts, but there have yet to be many major country performers from outside of English-speaking North America.

The work themes found in all of the various genres were generally common in terms of what artists wrote. The drudgery of work, having to get up and be on the job every day, and the experience of making life compromises for family reasons were found across genres. Work and labor were referenced in key songs, but personal relationships remained the most common theme. A song about work or a labor struggle can be enduring, but people want at least some escapism through music. This explains why so many people hear a patriotic song when *Born in the U.S.A.* is played, even though the lyrics question patriotism.

Notes

1 On the rise of the video rental business see Daniel Herbert, *Videoland: Movie Culture at the American Video Store* (Berkeley: University of California Press, 2004).
2 Merle Haggard, "Okie from Muskogee," recorded 17 July 1969, track 20 on *Okie from Muskogee*, 1969, vinyl LP.
3 Johnny Cash, "Folsom Prison Blues," recorded 30 July 1955, track 11 on *Johnny Cash with His Hot and Blue Guitar!*, 1957, vinyl LP.
4 Johnny Cash, "Oney," recorded 1972, track 6 on *Any Old Wind That Blows*, 1973, vinyl LP.
5 C.W. McCall, "Convoy," recorded 1975, vinyl single.
6 Johnny Paycheck, "Take This Job and Shove It," recorded 24 August 1977, track 1 on *Take This Job and Shove It*, 1977, vinyl LP.
7 Jerry Reed, "Eastbound and Down," released 1977, track 3 on *Smokey and the Bandit: Music from the Original Motion Picture Soundtrack*, vinyl LP.
8 Mel Tillis, "Sawmill," released 1983, track 7 on *Lack at Life*, 1983.
9 Glen Campbell, "Rhinestone Cowboy," recorded 24 February to 19 March 1975, track 6 on *Rhinestone Cowboy*, vinyl LP.
10 Loretta Lynn, "Coal Miner's Daughter," recorded 1 October 1969, track 1 on *Coal Miner's Daughter*, vinyl LP.
11 *Coal Miner's Daughter*, directed by Michael Apted, 1980; Los Angeles, CA: Bernard Schwartz.
12 Fraser McAlpine, "The unexpected origins of music's most well-used terms," 12 October 2018, BBC, https://www.bbc.co.uk/music/articles/dc64e24d-c4e7-4e34-b2f7-e34a00ea16ad.
13 The Eagles, *Hotel California*, Elektra/Asylum catalog no. 7E-1084, vinyl LP; The Eagles, *Their Greatest Hits (1971–1975)*, Asylum Records Catalog Number - 7E-1052.
14 The Eagles, "Take it Easy," released 1972, track 1 on *Eagles*, vinyl LP.
15 Jackson Browne, "The Load Out," recorded 27 August 1977, track 9 on *Running on Empty*, vinyl LP.
16 Styx, "Blue Collar Man (Long Nights)," recorded 1978, track 6 on *Pieces of Eight*, vinyl LP.
17 Bob Seger, "Feel Like a Number," released 1981, track 2 on *Stranger in Town*, vinyl LP.
18 Tina Turner, "Proud Mary," released 1970, track nine on *Workin' Together*, vinyl LP.
19 Kansas, "Dust in the Wind," recorded 1977, track 7 on *Point of Know Return*, vinyl LP.
20 Kansas, "Carry On Wayward Son," recorded 1976, track 1 on *Leftoverture*, vinyl LP.
21 Pink Floyd, "Money," recorded 7 June 1972 to 9 January 1973, track 6 on *Dark Side of the Moon*, vinyl LP.
22 Pink Floyd, "Welcome to the Machine," recorded 25 February 1975 to 28 July 1975, track 2 on *Wish You Were Here*, vinyl LP; Pink Floyd "Have a Cigar," recorded 10 March 1975 to 28 July 1975, track 3 on *Wish You Were Here*, vinyl LP.
23 Various, *Grease: The Original Soundtrack from the Motion Picture*, MMS ID 993340966305151, vinyl LP.
24 Frankie Avalon, "Beauty School Dropout," recorded 1987, track 6 on *Grease: The Original Soundtrack from the Motion Picture*, vinyl LP.

25 For an analysis of the rise and meaning of disco see Alice Echols, *Hot Stuff: Disco and the Remaking of American Culture* (New York: W.W. Norton, 2010).

26 Maristella Feustle, "Disco," in *The SAGE International Encyclopedia of Music and Culture*, ed. Janet Sturman (Thousand Oaks: SAGE, 2019), 738-740.

27 Rose Royce, "Car Wash," recorded 1976, track 1 on *Car Wash: Original Motion Picture Soundtrack*, vinyl LP.

28 Pat Lundy, "Work Song," recorded 1977, vinyl single.

29 The Village People, "Y.M.C.A.," recorded 1978, track 1 on *Cruisin'*, vinyl LP.

30 Various, *Saturday Night Fever: the Original Movie Soundtrack*, RSO – 2658 123, vinyl LP.

31 Various, *Flashdance: Original Soundtrack from the Motion Picture*, Casablanca – 422-811 492-1 M-1, vinyl LP.

32 Fred R. Shapiro, ed. *The New Yale Book of Quotations* (New Haven: Yale University Press, 2021), 524.

33 Troy Brownfield, "The Stooges Set the Stage for Punk 50 Years Ago With attitude, theatricality, and yes, raw power, The Stooges changed rock and roll," *Saturday Evening Post*, 9 August 2019, https://www.saturdayeveningpost.com/2019/08/the-stooges-set-the-stage-for-punk-50-years-ago/.

34 On the history of the Ramones see Donna Gaines, *Why the Ramones Matter* (Austin: University of Texas Press, 2018).

35 On the rise of the Sex Pistols and The Clash see Jon Savage, *England's Dreaming: Anarchy, Sex Pistols, Punk Rock, and Beyond* (New York: St. Martin's Griffin, 2002) and Marcus Gray, *Route 19 Revisited: the Clash and London Calling* (London: Jonathan Cape, 2009).

36 Steppenwolf, "Born to Be Wild," recorded 1968, track 5 on *Steppenwolf*, vinyl LP.

37 Stuart Jeffries and Jared Schiller, "Black Sabbath's Tony Iommi on the birthplace of heavy metal – video," 11 July 2011, *The Guardian*, https://www.theguardian.com/music/video/2011/jul/11/black-sabbath-tony-iommi-video.

38 Black Sabbath, "War Pigs," recorded 1970, track 1 on *Paranoid*, vinyl LP; Black Sabbath, "Paranoid," recorded 1970, track 2 on *Paranoid*, vinyl LP; Black Sabbath, "Iron Man," recorded 1970, track 4 on *Paranoid*, vinyl LP.

39 *Grand Ole Opry*, created George D. Hay, 1925-present, WSM.

40 Dolly Parton, "9 to 5," recorded 1980, track 9 on *Anthology*, vinyl LP.

41 George Strait, "All My Ex's Live in Texas," recorded 23 September 1986, track 1 on *Ocean Front Property*, vinyl LP.

42 George Strait, "Amarillo by Morning," recorded 1982, track 9 on *Strait from the Heart*, vinyl LP.

43 Farm Aid, "About Us," accessed 18 November 2023, https://www.farmaid.org/about-us/.

44 Raina Douris, "The First 100 Videos Played on MTV," 30 July 2021, NPR, https://www.npr.org/sections/world-cafe/2021/07/30/1021813462/the-first-100-videos-played-on-mtv.

45 Bruce Springsteen, *Greetings from Asbury Park, N.J.*, Columbia – KC 31903, vinyl LP.

46 Bruce Springsteen, *Born to Run*, Columbia – PC 33795, vinyl LP.

47 Bruce Springsteen, *The River*, Columbia – PC2 36854, vinyl LP.

48 Bruce Springsteen, *Nebraska*, Columbia – TC 38358, vinyl LP.

49 Bruce Springsteen, *Born in the U.S.A.*, Columbia – CK 38653, vinyl LP.
50 Kurt Loder, "The Rolling Stone Interview: Bruce Springsteen on 'Born in the U.S.A.,'" *Rolling Stone*, 7 December 1984, https://www.rollingstone.com/music/music-news/the-rolling-stone-interview-bruce-springsteen-on-born-in-the-u-s-a-184690/.
51 Loder, "The Rolling Stone Interview: Bruce Springsteen on 'Born in the U.S.A.'"
52 Bruce Springsteen, "I'm on Fire," YouTube, accessed 10 November 2023, https://www.youtube.com/watch?v=lrpXArn3hII.
53 Bruce Springsteen, "Glory Days," YouTube, accessed 10 November 2023, https://www.youtube.com/watch?v=6vQpW9XRiyM.
54 Bruce Springsteen, *Tunnel of Love*, Columbia – OC 40999, vinyl LP.
55 Michael Jackson, *Thriller*, Epic – QE 38112, vinyl LP.
56 Bon Jovi, "Livin' On a Prayer," recorded 1986, track 3 on *Slippery When Wet*, vinyl LP.
57 Billy Joel, "Piano Man," track 2 on *Piano Man*, vinyl LP.
58 Bill Joel, "Allentown," recorded 1982, track 1 on *The Nylon Curtain*, vinyl LP.
59 Bill Joel, *Innocent Man*, Columbia – 38-04259, vinyl LP.
60 Billy Joel, "Uptown Girl," YouTube, accessed 10 November 2023, https://www.youtube.com/watch?v=hCuMWrfXG4E.
61 Loverboy, "Workin' for the Weekend," recorded 1981, track 1 on *Get Lucky*, vinyl LP.
62 Dire Straits, "Money for Nothing," recorded 1985, track 2 on *Brothers in Arms*, vinyl LP.
63 Huey Lewis and the News, "Workin' for a Livin'," recorded 1982, track 5 on *Picture This*, vinyl LP; Donna Summer, "She Works Hard for the Money," recorded 1983, track 1 on *She Works Hard for the Money*, vinyl LP; The Bangles, "Manic Monday," recorded 1985, track 1 on *A Different Light*, vinyl LP.
64 Jackson Browne, "Lawyers in Love," recorded 1981–1982, track 1 on *Lawyers in Love*, vinyl LP.
65 Bob Dylan, "Union Sundown," recorded 1983, track 6 on *Infidels*, vinyl LP.
66 Neil Young, "This Note's For You," recorded 1988, track 2 on *This Note's For You*, vinyl LP.
67 The Alarm, "Devolution Workin' Man Blues," released 1980, track 3 on *Change*, vinyl LP.
68 XTC, "Earn Enough For Us," released 1986, track 8 on *Skylarking*, vinyl LP.
69 R.E.M., "Finest Worksong," recorded 1987, track 1 on *Document*, vinyl LP.
70 Bob Marley, "Work," recorded 1980, track 5 on *Uprising*, vinyl LP.
71 The Police, "Man in a Suitcase," on *Zenyatta Mondatta*, recorded 1980, track 9 on *Zenyatta Mondatta*, vinyl LP.
72 The Police, "Synchronicity II," recorded 1983, track 6 on *Synchronicity*, vinyl LP.
73 JayQuan, "Remembering Keith Cowboy," accessed 5 November 2023, https://web.archive.org/web/20060317071002/http://www.furious5.net/cowboy.htm.
74 Sugarhill Gang, "Rapper's Delight," recorded 2 August 1979, track 6 on *Sugarhill Gang*, vinyl LP.
75 The Jubalaires, "Noah," YouTube, accessed 10 November 2023, https://www.youtube.com/watch?v=Wx0oU1OnHf8.
76 Blondie, "Rapture," recorded 1980, track 8 on *Autoamerican*, vinyl LP.

77 Run-D.M.C., "Hard Times," recorded 1983, track 1 on *Run-D.M.C.*, vinyl LP.
78 Grandmaster Flash, "We Don't Work for Free," Sugar Hill Records – SH 32025, vinyl single.
79 On the influence of heavy metal see Jeffrey Arnett, *Metalheads: Heavy Metal Music and Adolescent Alienation* (Abingdon: Routledge, 1996).
80 On the PMRC see Claude Chastagner, "The Parents' Music Resource Center: From Information to Censorship," *Popular Music* 18, no. 2 (1999): 179–192.

Conclusion

Work and labor themes were found throughout American films, television programs, and music during the 1970s and 1980s. There were at times some major changes in how work and labor were presented, while at other times there was more consistency with how working life was presented. Work was represented in a range of forms including paid and unpaid, legal and illegal, and across different sectors of the economy. All three forms of popular entertainment mirrored what was happening in wider American society and culture but did not always fully represent everyone living in the country during two important decades.

Film

Film as a medium did not experience considerable alteration during the 1970s and 1980s. The development of the VCR did not fundamentally alter the film industry. If anything, it created video rental as a new line of retail business and made it possible for studios to extend the life of a newly released film through video sales and rentals, and also made it possible to make back catalogs of older films available to consumers. The technology used to make films evolved from 1970 to 1989, particularly the special effects and sound incorporated into film series like *Star Wars*.

The genres of films that were popular during the 1970s and 1980s were much the same as they had been in the two preceding decades. Science fiction became more sophisticated, which was again very clear in the *Star Wars* film, but other genres like crime and comedy remained much as they had always been. Work and labor appeared more overtly or covertly depending on the film. Lead characters in the *Star Wars* films worked, and a lot of additional work seen in them was done by androids or background characters. All of the characters in *Alien* worked, even if trying to survive an alien monster became their main endeavor.

DOI: 10.4324/9781003384564-5

The military is seen as a workplace in Vietnam war films, and it is an occupation that can bring considerable hazards and lasting consequences. Police work is a consistently popular part of Hollywood films, as is the unofficial work engaged in by criminals. Police work was generally shown in 1970s and 1980s films as something more effectively done by heroic anti-heroes like Clint Eastwood's Harry Callaghan. The collaborative nature of policing was often absent from films.

Films depicting outsiders were an important aspect of the 1970s and 1980s films that included work. *Taxi Driver* is the leading example of a film about a person who works alone and chooses to live on the social fringe. Robert De Niro's Travis Bickle is shown working in a job that involves long hours, drudgery, low pay, and interaction with socioeconomically marginalized people. Bickle is a suspicious character, while Sylvester Stallone's Rocky Balboa is a marginalized individual to whom people can relate. Rocky embodied working-class alienation and aspiration, even if he was really Chuck Wepner.

Unionized workers enjoyed positive cinematic depictions during the 1970s, but they were gradually displaced in the 1980s. Seeing *Norma Rae* may not have necessarily induced workers to sign union cards and organize, but the film did portray organized labor and the role of women in unions in a favorable manner at a time when American unions were under increasing attack. Unionized workers were still appearing on screen at the end of the 1970s, but a 1977 attempt to enact a law to reform and improve federal labor law failed due to opposition from political conservatives and the business community. The 1980s ended with Michael Moore creating a damning indictment of corporate behavior in *Roger & Me*.[1]

There was a marked shift from the end of the 1970s into the 1980s away from films based on actual events to productions that were more escapist. Movies like *Norma Rae* and *Silkwood* received less attention from film studios than the next installment in a blockbuster franchise. Professional workers were more prominent in 1980s films as the realism of the 1970s director's decade gave way to films that were more about simply entertaining people. The role of corporations in American life was often negatively portrayed on film, indeed a potentially dystopian society ruled by corporations had already been seen in *Rollerball*. Films like *Wall Street* depicted corporate and personal greed and gave viewers insights into how financial markets functioned. There were sometimes perception problems with a character like Michael Douglas's Gordon Gekko becoming an inspirational cultural icon for people who wanted to believe that greed is indeed good. Working women were leading characters in films about work in the 1970s and 1980s beyond *Norma Rae*. Films like *9 to 5* and *Working Girl* used humor to depict the challenges that women faced in office work.

Television

Television was also not significantly disrupted by technological change in the 1970s and 1980s. The introduction of cable networks, which were first called Community Antenna Television, was the main innovation to occur before the 1970s. Cable was developed to address reception problems faced by TV owners who used roof-mounted antennas. The three main American networks dominated broadcasting in the 1970s and 1980s, and they broadcast over cable and antennas. Work and labor appeared in popular series in both decades, with the 1970s being a period of particular prominence for working people on screen.[2]

When considering the 1970s programs that incorporated considerable content about working life, it is easy to describe those years as the decade of Norman Lear's working people. *All in the Family* and its spinoffs depicted everyday people who were working class, with the exception of *Maude* and *The Jeffersons*. The same kind of characters appeared in *Happy Days* and its spinoff shows. The 1970s were a period of showing everyday people performing average work, and often in humorous stories. All of the Lear programs, *Happy Days* and related shows, and the *Mary Tyler Moore Show* and its spinoffs were comedies. They incorporated narratives on race, gender, and class that viewers grasped because of the humor that was used by the various creators of the shows. There were shows that did not do well despite the best efforts of their creators. For instance, in 1984 Lear co-created a show called *a.k.a. Pablo* that starred Paul Rodriguez and was about a Mexican-American man trying to make a living as a comedian and his family dynamics; it only lasted for six episodes.[3]

Programs that were based on policing, protective services, and crime were usually dramas but there were a few exceptions to that pattern. Shows like *Hawaii 5-0* were meant to appeal to baby boomer audiences. Some of the series produced showed characters in more realistic living and working circumstances, such as the *Rockford Files*, while others like *Charlie's Angels* and *Magnum PI* were essentially escapist fare that gave viewers a break from their own routine working lives.

Programs made in other countries were not aired on the three major American networks—English-language programs made in other countries were generally relegated to Public Broadcasting (PBS) stations—and American networks instead made their own versions of them. This was evident with *Sanford and Son* being based on the United Kingdom's *Steptoe and Son*. American television programs diverged from those in other countries when it came to soap operas. That television format was perhaps the most escapist genre of any made in the United States in the post-World War II decades. Most of the characters in all of the soap shows lived in financially comfortable circumstances, some seemed to have jobs, but they otherwise devoted most of their time to relationship scheming. This was an enormous contrast with an overseas show like the United Kingdom's *Coronation Street* in which everyone worked and was often employed in blue-collar jobs.

Professional workers became a greater focus of the attention of television producers in the 1980s. Medical dramas were already popular before the decade began and shows like *St. Elsewhere* strove to provide a realistic portrayal of working in a hospital. Others like *LA Law* were less about realism and more about escapism, because while the show endeavored to be accurate in terms of how the legal profession operates, it showed wealthy lawyers leading comfortable lifestyles. *The Cosby Show* used humor to depict the home life of wealthy Black professionals. *Cheers* was one of the few shows to depict characters from different class and occupational backgrounds routinely interacting with each other.

Music

The music industry experienced technological disruption in the 1970s and 1980s compared to film and television, and it also experienced the rise and fall of new genres. This latter aspect of the industry is notable because film genres were established before the 1970s and did not alter into the 1980s, and television would not see a new genre until the rapid rise in popularity of reality programs in the late 1990s. Film goers and television viewers basically sat in theaters and in front of TV screens at home much as they had done in the 1950s and 1960s, although with more content from which to choose.

Music was also different from film and television because of influences from outside the United States. British bands were influenced by early American rock and roll, and they in turn influenced American bands. Reggae came from Jamaica and appealed to American music fans. Country music was really the only quintessentially American genre that did not quickly show direct influences from overseas, although a line can be drawn from country to folk music and that genre had European and African influences. For instance, the banjo is often ubiquitous in country songs and it originated as an African instrument.

Someone wanting to listen to music could listen on a 33 1/3 RPM LP, a 45 RPM single, a cassette tape, an eight-track tape, or a compact disc. The CD rose in popularity in the late 1980s, and its introduction had actually been intentionally delayed by the music industry. The eight-track tape had fallen out of favor by that time. Music listening devices because more portable with people being able to listen at home, in their cars, or even while wearing a Walkman or carrying a large boom box system. Film and television formats were not nearly as portable compared to music formats. Recording technology improved from the early 1970s to the late 1980s, and the emergence of MTV and music videos transformed the recording industry.

Work and labor themes were found in all music genres in the 1970s and 1980s, with some artists creating work that particularly focused on working life. Country artists like Johnny Paycheck and George Strait commented on the daily grind and struggle of work, Dolly Parton wrote and performed an anthem for working women everywhere with "9 to 5" and Loretta Lynn sang about growing up poor with a coal miner for a father. Farming was in crisis in the 1980s even though food production was robust in the United States and musicians including Neil Young, Willie Nelson, and John Mellencamp organized benefit concerts to help average family farms with their financial challenges.

Several rock and roll acts wrote and performed songs about working life, and those works included commentary on being a musician on the road. Jackson Browne and Neil Young described performing and traveling, which gave music fans at least some insight into actually working in the music industry. The 1980s were a period of industrial decline in the United States and Billy Joel, Bruce Springsteen, and Bob Dylan wrote enduring songs about the impact of globalization and the loss of good blue-collar jobs. Springsteen became closely associated with the de-industrialized north-east and the negative impacts of economic change on working-class Americans. So many of his songs, from "The River" to "Glory Days", were about alienation and loss. Springsteen was also not alone in seeing the meaning of his songs misinterpreted.

Heavy metal songs infrequently touched on work and labor themes, but they had firmly working-class roots. Metal also readily showed trans-Atlantic influences, as early British metal bands were influenced by American rock, and they in turn influenced the development of American metal acts. Metal was further divided into sub-genres, and the music was often full of alienation and even despair. It principally appealed to white working and lower middle-class young men who felt alienated from society, and metal bands were overwhelmingly white and male.

Metal rose during the 1970s and endured beyond the 1980s, but other genres had less endurance. Disco was primarily a creation of the 1970s and it was largely made possible by advances in recording technology. Some disco songs, like "Carwash", talked about working life but disco was otherwise meant to be an escape from daily toil. The *Saturday Night Fever* soundtrack was the primary exception to that trend. The songs on it were not about work, but the movie that it accompanied was all about one person's struggle to escape the confines of a low-wage job and limited personal prospects.

Punk arrived and departed even more quickly than disco, and really peaked in the second half of the 1970s. It was yet another genre with trans-Atlantic origins. Some songs touched on work themes but much of it was social commentary, with the British bands being more overtly political than their American counterparts. New wave arrived in the early 1980s and it maintained popularity after the 1980s, with performers like Duran Duran enjoying huge success. New wave acts created songs with work themes, and it was also at times escapist. It was a genre that benefited enormously from the development of music videos.

Some genres seemingly appeared out ether—including punk—and hip-hop was initially viewed on those terms. It grew increasingly popular between its appearance in the late 1970s and the end of the 1980s and expanded even more in later decades. Hip-hop was rooted in Black American culture, and it included songs that described the urban work experience. Feelings of alienation and defiance were seen in hip-hop lyrics, much as in music created by metal acts.

Looking for Work and Labor in the 1970s and 1980s

American working life was found throughout three key forms of media in the 1970s and 1980s: film, television, and music. Some creative work that incorporated work and labor themes has proved enduring, such as the songs of Bruce Springsteen. The television programs of the 1970s and 1980s now mainly exist on speciality streaming services or YouTube, along with most of the films made during those years. Music may have been the entertainment form altered the most by technological change, but it remains the most accessible.

There were inherent biases in representations of working people in film, television, and music. Most of the people who created content were white men. There were some exceptions including musicians like Dolly Parton and Tina Turner and there were a few women who produced television programs like *All My Children*, which was created by Agnes Nixon. The major films made in the 1970s and 1980s were directed by men. Content by Black artists like Spike Lee and those creating hip-hop music emerged in the 1980s.

Hollywood and the music industry ultimately want to tell stories that have happy endings. Working-class life was ultimately portrayed positively in films, television shows, and music. The hopelessness and full impact of poverty were not often portrayed in American popular media. Content creators depicted workers engaging in some protest, but who were otherwise agreeable and unthreatening. Workers were not often shown engaging in militant action on the job. Indigenous Americans were rarely seen on screen or in music, with the exception of productions like the period mini-series *Centennial*. LGBTQ characters were also rarely seen on screen or openly heard in music; the Village People broke new ground. Rank-and-file workers became more diverse in film, television, and music but their bosses mostly continued to be white men.[4]

The challenges and opportunities of working life are found in all three mediums. Technological change, globalization, the decline of unions, gendered work, race on the job, corporate behavior, and generational change are all seen in films, TV shows, and music. On one hand, there should have been more work and labor content considering the high levels of unionization in Hollywood. The music industry is much less unionized in comparison to movies and TV. On the other hand, the entertainment industry in the United States is overwhelmingly controlled by corporations and entertainment executives ultimately approve or reject content. A person, regardless of income or occupation, could sit in a theater, turn on a TV, put on an album and be exposed to creative content that related to their daily working lives. It is just a matter of sometimes having to look and listen more carefully to see the story of workers being told.

Notes

1 Jason Russell, *Management and Labor Conflict: An Introduction to the US and Canadian History* (New York: Routledge, 2023), 64.
2 For a history of the development of cable television see Patrick R. Parson, *Blue Skies: A History of Cable Television* (Philadelphia: Temple University Press, 2008).
3 *a.k.a. Pablo*, created by Norman Lear and Rick Mitz, 1984, ABC.
4 *Centennial*, created by James A. Michener, Charles Larson, John Wilder, and Jerry Ziegman, 1978–1979, NBC.

Index

For Product Safety Concerns and Information please contact our EU representative GPSR@taylorandfrancis.com
Taylor & Francis Verlag GmbH, Kaufingerstraße 24, 80331 München, Germany

www.ingramcontent.com/pod-product-compliance
Ingram Content Group UK Ltd.
Pitfield, Milton Keynes, MK11 3LW, UK
UKHW021822240425
457818UK00006B/39